Praise for *A Mosaic Heart*

With her highly personal style of writing, Terry Jones-Brady takes us into the innermost parts of herself as she experiences heartbreaking losses that shatter every notion of the life she thought she would live—creating a happy family with her husband and children. Jones-Brady writes with truth where there is no sentimentality or sense of being a victim, which comes from her deep roots and explorations of Source and Mystery that open her to a personal relationship with her God. *A Mosaic Heart,* with quotes from the plays of William Shakespeare beginning each chapter, can have meaning for all of us as we navigate our own unpredictable lives with losses and unfulfilled dreams and ask ourselves the questions of who we really are and how can we live fully the lives we have been given.

Eleanora Woloy, MD, DMin,
Diplomate Jungian Analyst

Terry Jones-Brady has endured more hardship than most of us could imagine, and her book, *A Mosaic Heart,* is a testimonial to the resilience of the human spirit and the human community. I hope that all who read it can learn from her story and follow her example of using grief as a spiritual path.

Gregg Korbon, MD, author of
Beyond Reason: Lessons from the Loss of a Gifted Child

In this wonderful book, Terry Jones-Brady courageously shares her extremely painful and powerful journey with us, inviting us to enter a new level of consciousness—a soul consciousness. By sharing her "shattered shards, reassembled with new love," Terry beckons us to follow. As a new time fast approaches, books like this will serve a vital function, leading us to a new level of faith and grace upon our earth.

David McMillian, LPC, LMFT,
host, *Strategies for Living* radio program

Terry Jones-Brady captures the essence of what it means to live with a savage grace. The story she tells is about more than resilience. It is about transformation and the opportunities that suffering offers for newfound wisdom and spiritual growth. *A Mosaic Heart* speaks about inner strength and the ways in which we can all help one another heal [during] life's inevitable losses. It is a book that you will return to again and again.

Kathleen Brehony, PhD, author of *Awakening at Midlife, Ordinary Grace, After the Darkest Hour,* and *Living a Connected Life*

A Mosaic Heart

Reshaping the Shards of a Shattered Life

Terry Jones-Brady

Some names of persons in this book have been changed, but the conversations and events depicted are true to the best of the author's memory.

Cover design by Jane Hagaman
Cover mosaic created by Terry Jones-Brady and photographed by Tania Seymour
Cover background image by iStockPhoto.com / Melissa King
Interior design by Jane Hagaman
Photos on pages 218–220 courtesy of Children's Hospital of the King's Daughters

Quartet Books
PO Box 4204
Charlottesville, VA 22905

If you are unable to order this book from your local bookseller, you may order directly from the author.
757-255-2102
www.terryjones-brady.com

Library of Congress Control Number: 2011913538

ISBN 978-0-615-51720-9

10 9 8 7 6 5 4 3 2

Printed on acid-free paper in Canada

For Heather and Holly

Contents

Acknowledgments

So many people have supported me throughout the writing of this book that I hardly know where to begin.

First, the learned women at Quartet Books—Jane Hagaman, Cynthia Mitchell, Tania Seymour, and Sara Sgarlat—thank you so much for all your help.

Next, special thanks go to Alva Moore, who read and critiqued my next-to-last draft with thoroughness above and beyond the call of friendship.

Thank you to Kerry Dougherty, *Virginian-Pilot* columnist, who awarded First Place for Non-Fiction at the 2010 Hampton Roads Writers Conference to my submission that became a chapter in this book. Winning that award encouraged me to keep on telling my story.

My friends and fellow writers at the Muse Writers Center in Norfolk, Virginia, have graciously read much of this book in many versions—Gerrie Beck, the late Bob Chorush, Linda Cobb, Cathy Collins, Dr. Maura Dollymore, Suzanne Dutton, Kelly Hardy, Lauren Hurston, Una MacGillivray, Leslie Piercy, Rachel Thompson, Mae Lynn Walker, and especially Lisa Hartz—thank you all.

Thank you to Dr. Eleanora Woloy, MD, who not only helped me to stay relatively sane, but also encouraged my writing for many years. And thanks to Eleanora and the rest of the women's group—Mary Fran Callahan, Sr. Nancy Healy, Mary Anne Henry, and Anne H. Prince—who provide my monthly spiritual touchstone.

Thank you to Kacey Carneal, whose cheerful paintings were a gift during the darkest of times at the hospital in Charlottesville and who has believed in this project from the beginning.

Thank you to Kathleen Brehony, PhD, who read the earliest drafts of the book and mentored me.

I'm grateful to Sharon Krumpe, PhD, Susan Reed, and Marcia Lynch, who picked up the slack at the counseling center when I left to concentrate on this work.

My thanks to Glenda Lanehart, Peg Hoagland, and Rusty McBride for understanding when I announced I was leaving our foursome until I finished *A Mosaic Heart.*

To my sister Emmy Martinez, my gratitude for her constant friendship and support.

To a whole family tree of Joneses, McKameys, Dodsons, Tyndalls, Hewetts, Reeds, and Martinezes, who loved and grieved along with me.

And most of all, my thanks belong to my beloved husband, Kevin W. Brady, without whose unwavering love and enthusiasm *A Mosaic Heart* might never have come to fruition.

Prologue

In my heart's core, ay, in my heart of heart . . .

—*Hamlet,* act 3, scene 2

Many years after my tragedies were over and done with, and after I was happy beyond my dreams, the idea came to me to make mosaic artwork. A mosaic artist can take bits and pieces of trash and treasure and create something beautiful. Fragments from Mother's bone china dinner plate that someone had dropped after too much Thanksgiving Day wine. Great-grandmother's brooch that she wore when she traveled in steerage from Ireland. The opal ring that had chipped when someone was trying to open a stuck window. All of these things and more can be used: buttons, shells, splintered stained glass, shattered ceramic tile—all arranged with an eye to visual appeal and configured into beautiful works of art.

My own heart had been shattered, broken into many pieces too many times. But the brokenness made room for light to shine into the cracks, mending like glue, refashioning my heart into a vessel capable of greater love.

So when a little voice in my head asked, "Why don't you make mosaic pieces?" I did. First, I smashed a set of blue-and-white plates patterned with tall ships. There were six plates in the set, and I no longer wanted either ships or blue dishes in the kitchen. I used the shards of the blue-and-white dinnerware to mosaic a square table for the gazebo. It looks like a table for four set with broken dishes and grouted lines. The table has a fruit basket centerpiece, also made from broken crockery, and a background of curvy lines constructed with tiny pieces of round and square tiles.

Next came a birdbath with glass goldfish and koi set in black grout. Then some wall hangings—pond-themed pieces for a bathroom that's decorated with water lily wallpaper. Then I tiled a small desk and the island in the kitchen. I constructed a mandala on the bottom of a large clay saucer using old costume jewelry, pieces of glass, and small round tiles.

My largest and most challenging piece was a picnic table anchored by a cheerful shining sun surrounded by cracked dinnerware place settings and coasters. Black grout unifies the piece. Around the edges of the picnic table, I put medium and large black and bronzed tiles. Stars and moons sprinkle and sparkle against the black background.

It's always a meditative experience to do these pieces, and one day this thought came to me: these projects have all been symbols of the inner mosaic I've made from the fragmented shards of my heart.

One thing's for sure. If you live on this planet long enough, your heart will be broken. The broken heart can be powerful. The broken heart has more room for more love. I found this out. Restoring the heart requires perseverance and spiritual work, but if I could do it, anyone can.

This story contains some material that is graphic in its description of terminal illness. I hope it won't offend. It's my raw material, my primary resource. My intent is not to share horror, but to demonstrate that redemption, renewal, and happiness can occur in our lives even after almost inconceivable tragedies. Please be patient. This story is a message of hope, despite desperately sad chapters. There will be happy reading, too. That's a promise.

Briefly, I need to explain the spiritual perspective from which I write. My heritage and upbringing are Christian, but my journey has not been constrained by a narrow religiosity or denominational doctrine. It was through faith in God that I sustained myself during the tragedies and worked through the grief. I respect all spiritual paths whose genesis is love. I've found solace and succor in aspects of other traditions, notably my practice of yoga as a physical/mental discipline, the understanding of suffering found in Buddhism, and in my study of ancient mythologies and the archetypal patterns explored and explained by the Swiss psychoanalyst Carl Jung.

These studies don't dilute my belief in the redemptive power of the Christ. On the contrary, they enhance my faith and my understanding of biblical teachings. In fact, much of my study of these traditions has taken place at church workshops and Christian retreat centers. An ecumenical spirituality gives a broader, deeper understanding of truth. The study is lifelong and never-ending.

At some point in my life I learned not to make into catastrophes events that comprise living the life one is given. Grief and tragedies happen, and they bear down upon us with dreadful weight. Yet I believe that we can each respond like the deeply rooted, old-growth trees that surround my house. During hurricanes, blizzards, and ice storms, I've watched the trees—oaks, beeches, maples, dogwoods, sweet gums, yellow poplars, hollies, pines, and cedars—bend and bow but rarely break. Almost always after storms, they respond to the call of the sun's rays and the nurturance of spring rains, growing taller and stronger every year.

I stand as proof that the human spirit is capable of responding to suffering with just such resilience.

Part One

CHAPTER ONE

Tim and Me

Journeys end in lovers meeting.

—*Twelfth Night,* act 2, scene 3

Tim and I fell in love under an oak tree one night, late, after a performance at a dinner theater. He was producing director, and I was a member of the cast. The play was *A Shot in the Dark.*

We met at an audition in New York City, where I'd moved after graduation from the University of California at Berkeley. Each morning, I walked down five flights of stairs from my rent-controlled apartment in the upper east side of Manhattan to attend open casting calls. It was important to hone my craft, so I took acting lessons, voice lessons, and dance lessons. During the few years that New York was home base, I worked as a summer stock apprentice at the La Jolla Playhouse, joined the cast of the Barn Dinner Theater near Charlotte, and appeared in a way-off-Broadway

Japanese-style theater production called *Zeami.* All those gigs were small potatoes, but necessary for gaining experience and building a résumé. My very favorite was the Utah Shakespeare Festival.

The summer in Cedar City, Utah, was vibrant. The festival was a repertory ensemble, producing three plays in rotation during the summer season. Most of the company performed in all three plays. We each got a major role in one, a secondary role in another, and a walk-on in the third. I played Regan in *King Lear,* Margaret in *Much Ado about Nothing,* and a servant in *The Merry Wives of Windsor.* It was fun and challenging to be afforded that versatility. Sir John Gielgud, one of the most famous Shakespearean actors of the twentieth century, was a member of the Honorary Board of Directors. Sir John wrote a nice letter to our managing director wishing us a successful season. That sent our company of young performers over the moon! Several years after my summer there, the festival was the recipient of America's Outstanding Regional Theatre Tony Award, a thrill for the festival and for its alums.

Celebrate Fifty Years: The Utah Shakespeare Festival, is a commemorative coffee-table book chronicling the festival's history. Recently I discovered that it contains a picture of me performing King Lear's cruel daughter, Regan. I'm on stage watching the Duke of Gloucester bleeding into his hands. Regan's husband, the Duke of Cornwall, stands by with a bloody sword. Cornwall had just blinded Gloucester. My red hair is braided and wrapped around a pale, haughty, mask-like face, and I wonder how the young girl that I was then had the empathy for Shakespearean tragedy. Probably, she did not. I had a good director who coached me into the role.

Producing a good play is a collaborative effort involving many unsung heroes—besides director and actors, there are set designers and builders, lighting designers, costumers, properties crew, and a stage manager. Every actor knows that her concept of the character she's portraying and the director's vision must result in a harmonious ensemble. A good director will motivate an actor, stretching her by means of suggestion and instruction, to become better than she thought she could be.

In repertory theater, we learned to work together, live together, eat together, and play together. I made long-lasting friendships, and one of the company members became my roommate for the remainder of my time in New York.

Besides acting, while I was in New York, I worked at the Canada Dry exhibit in the Better Living Center Pavilion of the World's Fair in Queens. I was aWink girl. We Wink girls wore cute outfits, smiled, and promoted a new soft drink called Wink. I also typed for temporary secretarial agencies to make ends meet. Some of it seemed glamorous to me at first. Some of it was fun. Much of it was hard work.

My heart had already been fractured in a love affair gone terribly wrong. At nineteen, I'd found myself dumped by a man whom I thought would love me forever. I spent too much time trying to fill the cracks with more of the wrong guys. After I was used and abused by the man who was old enough to be my father, my own father said, "Maybe marriage is not for you." Dad's implication: "Who would want you? You're damaged goods." Father was good at insulting his wife and daughters; he'd developed a divide-and-conquer strategy that set us at odds with one another.

Then along came Tim, presenting me with the opportunity to return to Virginia, where I was born and where my ancestors had lived for three hundred years until my father's gypsy ways took us thousands of miles away. Craving roots, tired of pounding Manhattan pavements, unwilling to return to California to my prickly family, I signed on as a company member with the Cavalier Dinner Theater in Norfolk. It was the heyday of the dinner theater as an entertainment venue, and Virginia had several. There was Barksdale near Richmond, Wedgewood in Williamsburg, and Cavalier in Norfolk—all of them prospering. "You're a Virginian. Go back to your origin," my inner guidance prompted.

The night I fell in love with Tim under the oak tree, he told me about his newest dream. He was going to start his own theater, build it from the ground up with a restaurant in the same facility but separate from the performing arts section. There would be two theaters in the building: a smaller one for experimental productions and a larger one for major shows.

"I honestly believe it'll be the most exciting theater venture between Atlanta and New York," he told me.

A mockingbird sang for its mate in the oak tree. We sat in silence for a while, listening.

Tim said, "Do you know that mockingbirds can sound like any other bird in the world?"

"Maybe I do."

Then he drew me into his arms and covered my face with kisses.

"This man is my destiny," my silent heart said, opening, beginning to sing.

"Will you marry me?" he asked.

"Maybe I will. Just once."

He kissed me some more. His beard tickled me. In 1966, few men in Virginia wore beards. His hint of unconventionality appealed to me.

Tim traveled to Manhattan to audition actors for his next show and brought back a Tahitian black pearl mounted with diamonds and set in white gold for my engagement ring. We were not traditionalists.

In those early days, it seemed that Tim was perfect, linking all the disparate elements of my experiences, upbringing, and desires. A man of intellect and humor, a Carolina gentleman, a poet, he charmed me with his warm, sensual charisma and his tender heart. Brilliant and consummate theater artist and director, yet without affectation. He was also an outdoorsman, lover of woods and water, virile and strong. His deep family roots called to the vestiges of family ties in my own psyche. I coveted the home I'd never really had. Tim was the one I could trust to fulfill my needs, to soothe my hurts, to fill my dark heart with his visionary radiance.

Keenly, I recall my first visit to his family home in a fishing village on the shores of Bogue Sound. The house was a modest white frame firmly planted in the coastal plains of eastern North Carolina. I sat across from my future mother-in-law at her kitchen table. She was a solidly built woman, short and unadorned. She wore an apron over her cotton housedress. I viewed her reverentially. Being with her took me back to the time in my earliest memory when life was rooted and stable, not the quasi-nomadic lifestyle I'd lived with my parents, but the treasured milieu of my grandparents.

I saw her as the mythic Greek Hestia, keeper of the hearth and home, usually in the kitchen preparing offerings of pork-seasoned greens, cornbread, and patted-out biscuits for her family. Barely graying hair tucked into a simple back-of-the-neck bun framed a solemn face. The hairdo and the face remained, most likely, as they had for many years. No pampering, no frivolity for this country housewife, the mother of my lover and of eight other babies, all born in a twenty-two year span. Tim was her baby, the youngest of them all.

We sat at the kitchen table, and she told me the sad story of Horace, her firstborn child.

"The shrimp boats were in," she began. "I left Horace with a neighbor lady named Ada so I could walk down to the fish house to get some shrimp to fix for supper."

She pronounced it "feesh" house.

"I was pregnant with Louise, and carrying Horace along with a mess of shrimp seemed too heavy. He was eighteen months old.

"Directly, Ada came flyin' down the road. 'Dodie, Dodie,' she hollered. 'Your youngern drank some kerosene and he's cryin' bad. I'm sorry, I'm sorry. I'm real sorry.' I pushed past her and raced to Ada's. My baby was lyin' on Ada's girl's lap, having fits, his head twisted back and his bowels comin' out from his bottom like pea soup.

"I grabbed Horace and sent May Ellen, Ada's oldest girl, down to the feesh house to get Ed quick as he could get here.

"'Ed,' I bawled at my husband when he ran in the door. 'Go to Morehead and get the doctor. Horace is bad off.' Ed set out runnin'. It was twelve miles to town. I prayed the Lord would send someone to give him a ride. And I pleaded to the Lord to heal my baby.

"By the time Ed and the doctor got back in the doctor's

car, I had the baby sittin' up, and I was spoonin' sweet ice tea into his mouth. He was gettin' his focus back, I could tell.

"The doctor had been drinkin'. I could smell it on his breath. But we were country people. Back in those days, I wouldn't dare say anything. He poured some paregoric into Horace's mouth and said, 'He'll be fine by tomorrow,' and he took off, leavin' the paregoric bottle.

"In just a little while, Horace stopped breathin'. I tried and tried to breathe my breath into his little mouth, but it didn't work. When the preacher came, he said it looked like the doctor gave him enough paregoric to kill a mule.

"For three days, I didn't eat and I didn't sleep. I was nineteen years old and expectin' another baby, but all I wanted to do was die and be with Horace.

"We buried the baby. After a while, the Lord helped me get back to everyday things."

I sat silent beside her. *How could a mother maintain her sanity after the tragic loss of her first child,* I wondered.

Tim was twenty-eight when his mother told me this story. His oldest brother would have been fifty. All those years after the death of her first baby, tears came to her eyes as she recalled the tragedy. My heart caught in my throat as I wondered how any woman could survive the loss of a child, any one of the children of her womb.

The air was thick and humid that September. Autumn's crispness hadn't yet come to eastern North Carolina. I wore a lavender and white sleeveless mini-dress, incongruous in this kitchen that hadn't caught up to the 1960s. The incomprehensibility of going on with life after the death of one's child—my mind couldn't grasp the enormity of that feat. I regarded my future mother-in-law with fearsome awe. Little did I know where life would lead me after I married Tim.

~

Tim's mother didn't entirely approve of his choice of the theater as a career.

While he was an undergraduate at the University of North Carolina, he wrote a play that was produced by the Carolina Playmakers.

His mother's only comment on opening night, after the applause and the accolades, was, "Son, I wish you hadn't used a curse word."

Tim's protagonist said "dammit" in one scene.

~

Back in Virginia Beach, we walked along the shore on a warm September afternoon—Tim with his beard, and me in a beach robe covering what may have been the first bikini worn on that conservative beach. Tired of the gypsy life, I was ready to put down roots, but I still loved the theater, and I'd found an exciting man, tall and elegant, with whom to share life, love, and Shakespeare.

"Let's live together in a cottage by the sea," he said.

We told our parents we were getting married. His mother's request: "Please get rid of that beard. I want a picture of you clean shaven on your weddin' day."

The ceremony was small and simple, on December 23. He wore a black suit and a shaved chin. I wore a short champagne-colored silk dress and gold shoes as a nod to the holiday season. I carried a spray of coral roses on a wooden diptych that portrayed a Renaissance wedding. It was Florentine gold painted and contained the inscription, "bless them with the love of their children's children." Tim had given me the artwork several weeks before the wedding.

We flew to California for our honeymoon, visited the Pasadena Playhouse where he had studied, and went to Disneyland, where—ever the showman—he tried to figure out the technology behind the cheery It's a Small World ride. We rented a car and drove down into Mexico, no passport required in those innocent, pre-terrorism days. On the way home from the West Coast, we were caught in the midst of a snowstorm in Atlanta. Our plane couldn't fly out, so the airline put us up in a hotel for an extra honeymoon night. After the warmth of Mexico and Southern California, it was sweet and unexpected to make love in a snug hotel room with snow falling outside the window.

We moved into our little seaside cottage, a guesthouse belonging to friends at the North End of Virginia Beach. Tiny and romantic, it had a living room and kitchen combination, a bedroom, and a bathroom. Tim continued to direct plays at several local theaters and moved ahead with the establishment of his own theater. I landed the role of Eliza Gant in Thomas Wolfe's *Look Homeward Angel* at the Little Theater of Virginia Beach, right there in our own backyard.

Between our own productions, we spent weekends in New York City and Washington, DC, going to the theater. On Broadway we cried at *Man of La Mancha* and laughed at Alan Alda in *The Apple Tree.* At the Arena Theater in Washington we saw *The Andersonville Trials* and met with the manager to discuss theater operations.

We slept late every morning, went to rehearsals in the afternoons, performed at night, and partied a lot. Together, Tim and I brought our version of the freewheeling 1960s culture of New York, where we met, and Berkeley, where I had lived for four years, into the time-honored traditions of southeastern Virginia. We began to study the works of Edgar Cayce and read books about reincarnation. Tim opened the Lake Wright Playhouse, later known as the Tidewater Dinner Theater of the Stars. Life was good.

After *Look Homeward Angel,* I was offered a part in *Twelfth Night* at the Virginia Beach Theater. I loved Shakespeare, but I loved Tim more. I chose to play Tiffany in his production of *Mary, Mary* instead of Olivia in *Twelfth Night.* The *Virginian Pilot*'s theater critic, in his review, called me a "chic New York import."

"The only thing missing from our lovely life is a baby," I said.

And soon I was pregnant. I was so thrilled that I began walking with my belly deliberately stuck out, swaybacked like an old brood mare. Pregnancy was enjoyable. I felt good and had lots of energy. I walked a lot to keep myself fit. Tim and I staged Bram Stoker's *Dracula* at the Playhouse. He was a handsome Count Dracula. Playing Lucy, I wore flowing gowns to hide my tummy, newly and truly emerging by then. Our costumer made two gowns, identical in style, one white and one black. I wore the white one until I fell into the clutches of the fanged Count. No longer the innocent virgin, Lucy changed into her black costume to writhe in sexual ecstasy as Count Dracula left fang marks on her pallid neck. It was a stylized, campy production, and we had great fun.

But the Playhouse was not making money. There was a huge mortgage to pay, the acting company was Equity, so we paid union scale wages, and we didn't have the funding to meet the overhead. As my pregnancy advanced, Tim was spending more and more time away from home, determined to make the theater work. I was alone a lot.

I decorated a nursery in a new little house we'd rented near the theater in Norfolk. With a baby on the way, the seaside cottage was too small. Anyway, he wanted to be nearer to the theater. The house we moved to had two bedrooms, hardwood floors, a stone fireplace, a stone exterior, shade trees in the yard, and a staircase going up to an attic. It was a happy place for me, at first.

We bought a golden retriever puppy. One day we couldn't find her. We panicked and searched the house. Finally, we located her wedged behind the sofa. She was very happy to see us, wagged her tail joyfully, and we breathed a mutual sigh of great relief.

Tim said, "Imagine what it would be like if we lost the baby!"

Neither of us could conceive of such a thing. We would have a perfect baby. She was going to be a girl; I knew it, even in those pre-ultrasound days. In my dreams, a little girl often came to visit me. In one dream, a girl rowed a small boat across a large lake to get to me.

"I am Ursula," she said.

"Would you like to name the baby Ursula?" I asked Tim when I woke up.

"No."

"Me neither, really."

The Playhouse spiraled further into the red. Tim began to drink too much. Before the pregnancy, we'd always partied. Almost every weekend there was a cocktail party somewhere that we attended, or a barbecue on the beach with plenty of beer on ice, or a Bloody Mary brunch, or an end-of-show cast party. We entertained a lot at our home, too, before I was pregnant. I began to worry about Tim's increasing solitary drinking, but I pushed my worries aside.

I was happily expecting our baby, and much in love with my husband.

One bright November morning I woke up and announced, "I'm going to have the baby today."

"How can you tell?" he asked.

"My back feels achy in a different way. I know the baby's coming."

Later, Tim was getting ready to leave the house. "I'll be at the theater. Call me if you're sure."

He was always at the theater. It was Sunday, and he had a rehearsal of the musical *Cabaret.* A couple of hours later, I was very sure. After speaking with the obstetrician, I called Tim. We drove to the hospital, both of us nervous. I vividly remember walking across the parking lot, hurting, leaning on Tim as he helped me endure the contractions that were becoming more frequent. The mid-afternoon sun cast a golden glow on our whole world in that dazzling way that can only happen in the autumn of the year.

Three hours later we had our new daughter.

CHAPTER TWO

Births and Deaths

. . . my mother cried, but then
there was a star danced, and under that was I born.

—*Much Ado about Nothing,* act 2, scene 1

We had chosen Heather for her name. Heather was the name of one of my high school friends. Such a pretty name, I'd thought, and so unusual. I'd made up my mind when I was sixteen—if I ever have a daughter, I'll name her Heather.

Recently, I searched online and found that in the decade of my birth, the popularity ranking of the name Heather was 970 out of 1,000. No wonder my friend was the only Heather in our large high school. In 1969, the year my daughter was born, her name ranked at 70 out of 1,000, and by 1974, Heather had risen to number four on the list of 1,000 baby girls' names. So much for originality. Yet she was a unique child. A tiny baby born at full term, but we had to leave her in the hospital a little longer than the typical three days, until her weight reached five pounds.

"We're discharging you this morning, but the baby can't go home yet," said the obstetrician. "She's too small."

"Oh, no! How will I feed her?" My eyes filled with tears.

"You can come back to the hospital every four hours, or you can pump your breasts. But to be honest, we don't recommend breast milk for such small babies. They grow faster on formula."

Not my baby, I thought.

Tim and I left the hospital without Heather. We didn't smile on that gloomy drive home, just the two of us. We were sad not to be fully a family of three quite yet, in the little house with its new nursery. My uterus was emptied, but my heart was full of the dream of a plump, bouncy baby snuggling at my breast. A friend drove me back and forth to the hospital several times every day to nurse my baby. I became exhausted and almost lost my milk. Heather was a week old when we finally brought her home.

Her eyes gazed at us with blue clarity. Even in infancy, they seemed filled with wisdom, as if they were the bright young eyes of an old woman. As she developed from an infant to a toddler to a little girl to a pre-teen, she was precocious. She read at three years old, was in special programs for the academically and artistically talented by second grade, and in the seventh grade, she was chosen to take the SATs and attend a summer program for talented youth at Johns Hopkins University. Of course, she didn't go to Johns Hopkins, because by the summer after seventh grade, she was dead. Still. . . .

~

Heather was afflicted with cystic fibrosis, an unwelcome and constant visitor in our household. Children with CF have a variety of symptoms—salty-tasting skin, persistent coughing, frequent lung infections, wheezing, shortness of breath, low weight gain in spite of a good appetite, and horrible stools. Her pediatrician noted the poor growth early on, and I mentioned her voracious appetite and messy diapers. When she was eight months old, he sent us to a lab for a sweat chloride test, because Heather was gaining so little weight even though she was eating well.

Tim and I had never heard of cystic fibrosis or a sweat chloride test, but we learned quickly. The sweat chloride test was and continues to be the definitive test for determining the presence of CF. Individuals who have the condition have a much higher than normal amount of chloride in their sweat.

Here's how the test was given to our tiny daughter. We took her to Virginia Beach General Hospital to the outpatient lab. A technician led us all into a procedure room where layers of hot wet toweling were wrapped around her arm. Then several layers of plastic were swathed around the wet towels, and it was all taped up into a cocoon meant to produce enough sweat from her thin arm to collect in a specimen cup and send off to be analyzed. She whimpered at first but calmed down as Tim and I stroked and soothed her. This sweat-inducing method was successful and the results of the test were positive for CF.

CF is a genetic disease that affects the respiratory and digestive systems of the body by making the normally thin mucus in each of these systems become thick and sticky. Although she was diagnosed and treated early for digestive problems, Heather's respiratory system was damaged irreparably by the time she was seven. We didn't know that until later. We took care of the stools and nutritional needs, but held out hope that her lungs would stay clear.

We didn't anticipate one thing leading to another as the cycle of the disease progressed. First, the thick, sticky mucus blocked the airways. This obstruction meant it was harder for her body to remove germs from the lungs, which led to infection. Thickened mucus created an environment for bacteria to grow and infection set in, which led to inflammation. White blood cells arrived and entered the lungs to fight illness. That's why a lab test for elevated white blood cells is used to diagnose infections. These white blood cells left behind a waste product that made mucus even stickier and led to more obstruction, more infection, more inflammation, and declined lung function. Initially, all this was going on so subtly that we didn't recognize the process.

Heather's first obvious signs of CF were the digestive problems, because pancreatic enzymes weren't available to her digestive tract. The problem was not that her pancreas wasn't manufacturing enzymes. The sticky mucus affected every organ in her body, blocking the pancreatic ducts of the pancreas and preventing the enzymes from reaching her intestines to aid digestion. Thus the constant diarrhea and failure to thrive that we saw during her first eight months of life. The very first thing we had to do was start feeding her enzymes. An enzyme supplement called Pancrease came in powdered form; we mixed it into a little applesauce and fed it to her prior to each meal or snack. Every day. All the time.

Pancrease helped her digest her food, but it also ate away at her skin when it came out the other end. The day after her first dose of enzymes, her previously smooth little bottom was red with an angry, puffy rash—another shock to my mother's heart. Diaper rash was distressing when I first saw it, but easier to deal with than the CF diagnosis.

Cornstarch helped clear up the rash. We settled in. Cystic fibrosis was with us for the long haul.

Our pediatrician made an appointment for us at a local Cystic Fibrosis Clinic. Tim said to me as I dressed Heather on the morning of our first clinic visit, "You don't want to be late."

I shrugged and said nothing. Heather and I went to that first appointment by ourselves. Maybe he didn't want to miss any work. More likely, he couldn't face what we might have to deal with. Very early in Heather's life with cystic fibrosis, I realized, albeit subconsciously, that I would probably have to be the stronger one in the family.

The clinic was situated in the basement of a building that was the first to house the Children's Hospital of the King's Daughters in Norfolk. The building was old and the clinic was cramped. The doctor who headed the clinic had a pediatric practice in the Newport News/Hampton area and came to Norfolk periodically to treat the CF kids there.

I met a few other families whose children had cystic fibrosis.

"Heather is basically a healthy little baby," the clinic doctor told me. "She's too young for chest physical therapy and doesn't need it now. Her main problem is her digestion. Just keep giving her the enzymes and bring her back in three months. She should be on a nonfat diet to help keep the diarrhea under control."

No one knew much about cystic fibrosis in 1970.

Tim and I agreed from the very beginning that our child

would have as normal a life as possible. We would not treat her as a hothouse flower.

The grandparents, aunts, and uncles on both sides were disturbed by the news. My mother cried and canceled a bridge game.

"I told my bridge partners our little granddaughter has just been diagnosed with cystic fibrosis," Mom said through her tears.

Tim had four sisters who loved us, but there was one who looked at everything in the most negative way possible.

The negative one sneered, "We all knew something was wrong with her. Her hips look so odd."

What a hurtful comment.

"Her hips?" I asked.

"Her hips are too small," said my sister-in-law of our baby, who was less than a year old.

True—she had tiny hips and a fat little belly, the result of the undigested food in her system. Tim and I were convinced that we could control the digestive problems with enzymes and proper (improper, we later discovered) diet. We were grateful that she had no respiratory involvement and actually believed in those early days that she never would.

When she was a few months older, maybe a year and a half, we were told to start putting her in a mist tent for sleep. The mist tent was a plastic contraption that enclosed the crib. It was attached to a nebulizer that sprayed a solution of sterile water and propylene glycol into the tent. The theory was that inhalation of the mist during sleeping hours would inhibit thickening of bronchial mucus and help to prevent infection.

The mist tent was noisy and wet. Heather woke up with her hair drenched in the glycol solution. Every day I had to sterilize the nebulizer and the mist tent by wiping them down with alcohol. We shampooed her hair every morning, and had it cut into a pixie style that was adorable on her tiny face.

Quarterly visits to the dreary CF clinic in the basement of the hospital continued.

Every three months I heard, "She's doing well and gaining weight. Keep doing what you're doing." This was the report we got at each clinic visit for the first few years.

Research told us that the average life span for children with CF was twelve years. Not long enough.

Tim and I attended a cystic fibrosis conference in Richmond. We met a doctor who specialized in the disease and taught pediatrics at the University of Virginia Medical Center. Heather was three, and we decided to make an appointment with him.

We took her to Charlottesville, to the University, where a series of tests and x-rays, including another sweat test, were administered. The sweat test at UVA was done differently. First, her arm was swabbed with a sweat-inducing chemical and then electrodes were placed on the skin of her forearm for about thirty minutes, gathering sweat.

She was amazingly cooperative for a three-year-old. No crying, no whining. We made it into a little bit of a game.

"Guess what, Sweetie? You get to have some magical buttons put on your arm so the doctor can see what's going on inside you. Lucky you—not many little girls get to do this."

"Is it gonna hurt?"

"Nope. Not at all."

"Okey dokey," she said.

The technician laughed as Heather sat on my lap sticking her little arm out for the new game.

The retrieved sweat was sent to the lab for analysis. Once again, the test was positive for cystic fibrosis. The doctor in Charlottesville said, "She has an ordinary, garden variety of CF. Nothing too serious in the lung area. Keep doing what you're doing."

He did, however, send us to physical therapy, where we were taught to do chest percussion and postural drainage as a precautionary measure. Respiratory therapists, patients, and parents referred to this technique as chest physical therapy, or CPT. We obtained a tilt table that could be slanted at angles of thirty to forty-five degrees. Heather was placed with her head at the lower point of the angle and her feet elevated, to allow gravity to drain her lungs. Specific positions enabled different lobes to drain. To facilitate the drainage, we used our cupped hands for clapping on various lobal areas to loosen secretions.

Tim's mother died when Heather was three. One morning shortly afterward, my daughter told me, "Grandma came to see me last night."

"What did she look like?"

"Like an angel, of course," she said, as if I'd lost my mind. "What else would she look like?"

Heather's first hospitalization occurred when she was three and a half years old, and it was unrelated to CF. One morning she awoke with a fever. Her skin was very hot to the touch.

"My neck hurts on the inside," she told me, pointing to her throat.

I called the pediatrician's office and took her in for an exam. The doctor took one look at her throat and said, "There's your problem. She has strep."

He prescribed an antibiotic, and we left the office. My

gut told me that was not the whole answer; nevertheless, I picked up the antibiotic and began giving it to her as directed. The next morning her fever was higher, she had an odor I'd never noticed before, and she held her body in an odd, rigid posture. We went back to the pediatrician.

Heather sat on the examining table with her legs flexed in front, her neck extended, and her arms behind her for support.

"Look at the way she's sitting," he said. "That's called a tripod posture, and it's a sign of meningitis."

"Can you smell the strange odor?" I asked him.

"I've heard of schizophrenia having an odor, but I've never heard of it in meningitis cases." He was trying to be funny.

But the smell was evident to me.

He admitted her to the Children's Hospital of the King's Daughters, where we'd been going for her quarterly CF clinic visits in the basement. This time we were upstairs in the inpatient section of the King's Daughters building.

Tim joined me at the hospital. Heather was taken to a procedure room for a spinal tap while we waited, both of us scared. We were told it could either be viral or bacterial meningitis. Bacterial meningitis was the more serious and could result in brain damage.

Fortunately, it turned out to be the viral form. Heather remained hospitalized for several days, and I stayed with her every minute, spending the nights on a cot beside her bed.

In the middle of one night, I was awakened by a young girl shaking my shoulder. She was a respiratory therapy student from a community college in North Carolina.

"The chart says you're supposed to do her chest physical therapy," she said.

"I volunteered to do it if no one else is available," I answered her, groggy.

"The only reason we're in a hospital like this is to get our hours in," she informed me, not without condescension as she left the room.

So at 2:00 a.m., I did Heather's CPT. I hadn't yet learned about patient and parent advocacy, but I did speak to the head nurse about it, and that was the last time I was awakened in the middle of the night by a respiratory therapy student.

Heather had a private room, but it had no bathroom. She had to go down the hall to a restroom with several pint-sized stalls.

"My wee-wee smells funny," she commented.

"It's the medicine you're taking, Sweetie."

One morning, she was in the girls' communal bathroom and had taken off her pajama top. Her pediatrician dashed into the restroom, eager to finish his rounds and get to his office.

Heather covered her small chest with her hands, protesting, "Mommy, he can see my breasts!"

The doctor laughed uproariously.

During that first hospitalization, I began to talk to the Virgin Mary in my prayer time. I talked to her statue in the hospital chapel. Lying on my cot at night, I visualized talking to her in person. I talked to her as one mother to another, knowing that she had watched her child suffer and die in a horrible manner, and I prayed for solace.

It may have been the day of the first sweat chloride test, or it may not have been until the first hospitalization that I knew I needed to find to some spiritual sustenance for our family. I was young and naïve and had left the Episcopal church of my childhood.

My childhood church, St. Andrew's Cathedral in Honolulu, was sedate and stately during the 1940s and '50s. My father sang tenor solo in the cathedral, served on the all-male vestry, and for ten years earned his living from the church. He was treasurer of the Missionary District of Hawaii, overseeing the finances of all the Protestant Episcopal churches in the Hawaiian Islands, Guam, Okinawa, Taiwan, and Kwajalein. His office was adjacent to the cathedral and in the same building as the bishop's office. My mother stitched sock dolls for the annual bazaar, ironed altar linens, and taught music to preschoolers at St. Clement parish nursery school. We were immersed in Anglicanism for most of my growing up years.

Tim had long since abandoned the rural southern Church of God in whose fervent zeal he was brought up. He had early childhood memories of lying on a hard wooden pew at evening services, trying to shut out the minister who was hollering about hellfire.

We both had the sense of a Power, simultaneously transcendent and imminent, with which I was beginning to become acquainted. I believed that the anchor we would throw out would not go into the muddied waters of traditional creeds.

I know it was during the first hospitalization that I realized, too, that I had to have another baby. I loved Heather so much, and I needed a second baby. My heart contained so much love, I needed to share it with another child.

Heather was discharged from the hospital. For a couple of days, our three-year-old walked around the house like a little old lady, crouched over from the stiffness in her lumbar spine caused by the spinal tap. Her bout with meningitis occurred in July. A month later, I was pregnant.

During the second pregnancy, I didn't have dreams of the baby to come as I had with Heather. I thought I would have a boy this time. I didn't expect the baby to have cystic fibrosis, although I knew that the disease was genetic and that each time Tim and I conceived there was a 25 percent chance our child would have CF. The odds were in our favor, we thought.

Others were not so optimistic. A pediatrician flat out told me, "We can't help you here, but you could go to Boston or Washington and get it taken care of. I'd be willing to give you the names of some doctors in those cities."

Is he talking about an abortion? I thought. *No, no, no! I want this baby!*

One of my best friends from college wrote to me: "You are a fool to have another child."

Her comment stung.

Ending the pregnancy was never an option for Tim and me, though I respect the right of a woman to choose her reproductive options. I wouldn't fault any woman for choosing an abortion in my circumstances, but I've never regretted my choice for one moment.

~

By the time of our second pregnancy, Tim had given up the Lake Wright Playhouse. Heather's condition and medical needs necessitated a more secure income with benefits and health insurance. Much to his credit, Tim acknowledged the growing responsibilities of parenthood and let go of his theater ambitions. Norfolk's Scope arena had opened and was followed by Chrysler Hall in the same complex. Chrysler Hall is a music and theater venue that was home to the Norfolk Symphony, now the Virginia Symphony Orchestra, as well as touring Broadway productions and other concert and theatrical events. Tim was hired by the City of Norfolk as manager and promoter of Chrysler Hall, and he coordinated its grand opening in the early 1970s.

My second pregnancy went smoothly. I didn't have quite the energy that I'd had during the first one, and I gained a bit more weight. I was, after all, four years older. Heather and I walked a lot around our Norfolk neighborhood and down by the Lafayette River. Despite the CF diagnosis, she was energetic, full of life, and showed a real creative streak. She loved creating artwork and making up dances. Beyond the meningitis scare, she was rarely sick. I remember one time she had a slight cold, and Tim said pleadingly, "Don't start coughing, Sweetie." We believed that as long as her lungs were not infected, all would be well with her. Please don't have a cough. Please.

We began attending a Unity Church during this second pregnancy.

When I first discovered Unity's teachings, I felt as if I had found a group that taught what I'd always believed. I found their doctrine positive, something I deeply needed; a progressive approach to Christianity based on the teachings of Jesus and the power of prayer. At the same time, Unity respected universal truths in all religions and each individual's right to choose a spiritual path. Tim was less enthusiastic about organized religion of any kind but joined me in attending the Unity services that were held in a Norfolk hotel while a church was under construction.

One morning, I went to my ob/gyn appointment. It was late in the pregnancy, and the obstetrician examined me. "You're not dilated at all. It will probably be a another week."

The next day, I began having contractions and pains in my lower back. I called the doctor's office.

"Those are Braxton-Hicks contractions," he said. "You won't go into labor for a few days."

I took Heather by the hand, and we started strolling through the neighborhood. Walking would relieve the false contractions, I had read. Later in the evening, I was kneeling on the bathroom floor giving her a bath when the contractions became severe. It was May 8 and my due date was May 10. I realized there was no way these pains were false labor. Heather went to a neighbor's house, and Tim took me to Norfolk General Hospital.

Once again, it took three hours for us to have a new daughter. I'd been expecting a little boy, and in my sedated state, I asked the doctor to please check again and make certain the baby was a girl. Everyone in the delivery room laughed, except me.

Tim, elated, said, "She weighs over seven pounds." We beamed at each other. No cystic fibrosis this time! We'd feared low birth weight as a sign of CF. Seven pounds and five ounces sounded perfectly large. Tim left the delivery room to make phone calls. When he returned, the nurse was cloaking my baby in receiving blankets. He watched, disturbed. He seemed angry.

"What's wrong?" I asked.

"Oh. Nothing."

Then the baby was put in my arms. My heart fluttered wide open. I stroked the wavy blond wisps of hair around the face of our new daughter, Holly Bailey. Then we went in three different directions—Holly to the newborn nursery, me to a room in the maternity unit, and Tim to pick up Heather and go home.

CHAPTER THREE

Good or Bad

There is nothing either good or bad,
but thinking makes it so.

—*Hamlet,* act 2, scene 2

The next morning, our pediatrician entered my hospital room, along with a nurse. I was sitting in a chair next to the bed. The doctor said, "We have a problem."

I blinked, frowned, felt sudden enormous trepidation. The nurse shoved a glass of water and a Valium tablet into my hand and said, "You need to take this."

Then the doctor said, "The baby has cystic fibrosis. We're transferring her to ICU at King's Daughters. She has a condition called meconium ileus, and that's a sure symptom of the disease. She might need surgery."

Meconium ileus is a condition in which the bowel matter (meconium) of the newborn is obstructed in an area of the intestine called the ileum. The physicians, nurses, and

Tim had all seen her distended belly at birth, but I hadn't. She'd been cleaned and wrapped quickly in the delivery room before she was given to me. I guess they all decided I needed a night's rest.

"Can't I nurse her?" I queried through falling tears.

"Let me see your breasts," he said. He really, really said that.

I lifted my gown.

He looked.

"You have great equipment." He said that! He did!

I had just given birth. I had just been told to bare my breasts. Hospital helplessness and patient intimidation, all that combined with heartbreak rendered me incapable of wondering about the appropriateness of his comment.

"I'll arrange for you to have a breast pump."

I was decimated.

Later that day I told a nurse I needed to pump my breasts to deliver milk to my baby. The staff seemed to have forgotten.

"Does your baby have the sucking reflex?" she asked.

Oh, how her comment hurt. Does the staff in this hospital know anything about cystic fibrosis? *Of course my baby has the sucking reflex,* I thought.

Cystic fibrosis has nothing to do with the sucking reflex in a full-term infant. The nurse seemed to think that Holly suffered from a neurological disorder.

"She has her sucking reflex," I said.

The next morning, the pediatrician said, "We've arranged for you to be admitted as a patient to Children's Hospital of the King's Daughters."

Thank goodness! I was placed in a room down the hall from ICU in the children's hospital, and Holly was brought to me for nursing. The nurses pasted Pancrease on my nipples to aid her digestion.

As I nursed Holly over the first few days of her life, and with the aid of the enzymes, the impacted matter passed naturally. I remain forever grateful for that. We took her home and placed her in a bassinette next to our bed. Now there were four of us, and we would make it work. We would take care of our daughters and their afflictions, and we would all live long happy lives together.

Our routine began: CPT and postural drainage for Heather twice daily. Pancrease for both children with every meal, snack, or feeding. Heather's appointments continued regularly at the cystic fibrosis clinic, where we were told to dispense with her noisy mist tent. About the time that Holly was born, studies showed that the mist tent was ineffective in reducing sputum viscosity. Thank God for that!

One night when Holly was nine weeks old, she began to cry, but her crying didn't sound like it usually did. She emitted a high-pitched squeal, an eerie sound. I lay in bed next to Tim with Holly cradled in my arms, encouraging her to nurse. She refused. It was late at night. Tim said, "Maybe we should call the doctor."

"No! He'll put her right back in the hospital. No, I won't call him!"

But after several hours of high-pitched squealing that diminished to soft baby moans, I realized something was desperately wrong. I rushed her to the pediatrician's office first thing in the morning. He took one look at her. "She's in shock. Has her belly ever been this distended?"

I shook my head.

"Call your husband, and take her straight to King's

Daughters." He handed me the phone, and I called Tim at his office.

I drove to the hospital just around the corner from the doctor's office. I sat down in the lobby at the end of a queue of patients and parents waiting for admission. I held Holly, who was no longer crying, tight to my bosom. Very soon Tim came dashing in.

"Why are you sitting here?'

"Waiting our turn to be admitted." He realized that I was in shock.

"We'll take her upstairs and admit her later." He was the strong and sensible one that morning.

He took Holly from me, and we dashed to the elevator. Our pediatrician had called ahead so they were expecting us. Immediately, a bevy of residents, interns, and nurses surrounded her. Holly was spitting up bile.

"We've got to act fast," said one of the residents.

From that moment on, my baby was almost completely out of my hands. For hours, then for days and weeks. First, we were ushered into a room in the hospital's bowels, where there were rows of little cribs. My memory of that earliest children's hospital is that it was a Dickensian place. A stationary heat wave over the area had knocked out electrical power. The hospital's backup generator had kicked in but certain procedures were delayed a bit. A pediatric surgeon came down to the dark, dingy ward with its rows of cribs and introduced himself.

"Her intestine has perforated, and the contents of the bowel are spilling into her abdominal cavity. We have a very serious situation. We're going to operate, and there's about a fifty/fifty chance she'll survive."

We were shuffled over to Norfolk General Hospital to

the surgical waiting room. King's Daughters didn't have its own operating rooms in 1974. I called my mother on the pay phone in the hallway to tell her that her namesake granddaughter was in surgery. Mom's maiden name was Bailey, a name that I thought would be lovely as a first name. Bailey Anne, I'd suggested, but Tim had disagreed. Hence, she was Holly Bailey. My parents lived in California, three thousand long miles away from us.

Mom said, "Oh, Honey. I knew something was wrong. I just got home from a bridge game. My car seemed to take me of its own accord toward home. I knew there had to be a reason—usually I run by the library and the market after the game. I thought it had to do with your father. You must be so terribly frightened! I'll call St. Aidan's and get the prayer chain started."

Our family on my mother's side has always had a sixth sense about one another, going back at least to my great-grandparents' generation and probably before. Her reaction didn't surprise me.

Tim called his sisters who lived in the area, and they came to the hospital to sit with us. I was wearing what I'd thrown on at dawn that morning—bellbottom jeans, platform sandals, and a yellow crop top shirt. One of my sisters-in-law yanked on the hem of my crop top, trying to make it cover the half inch of skin that was exposed above my waist. It was a rather modest crop top for the mid-1970s, more like a short tee shirt. But not acceptable to her.

She said, "I'm going to get you a cup of coffee. It'll relax you."

I thought a glass of wine would be a better relaxant, but I was still a nursing mother, and, anyway, wine was not on the menu in the hospital's cafeteria.

The other sister-in-law called her pastor at the Church of God, and I called our Unity minister. The hours dragged. It helped that there were people sitting with us.

The surgeon came into the waiting room. He looked grim. He wore his green scrubs and was smoking a cigarette.

Looking at Tim's sisters, Violet and Gwen, he asked, "Are these ladies family members?"

Tim nodded.

"We resected part of the ileum. The bowel was probably weakened in utero. The obstruction had most likely been there some time before birth. She has an ileostomy, and she'll be in ICU for a while. You can go to the ICU waiting room and see her soon."

I was numb; Tim was not, from the very start of this day.

"Families in Broad Creek who don't have a pot to pee in or a window to throw it out of have six or eight healthy little tattered kids running around barefoot," he said to me. Broad Creek is the name of the fishing village in which he was born and raised. He hugged me, and we shared our sense of calamity.

We walked through the tunnel connecting the two hospitals and rode the elevator up to the third floor. There, we sat in the small shabby waiting room outside the ICU until we were allowed to don hospital gowns and enter the unit, noisy with beeping machines and lit with shrill fluorescent overhead fixtures. Holly was asleep, hooked up to an assortment of tubes, with a pouch attached to her belly to collect waste and a nasogastric tube inserted into her nose for feeding.

The protective numbness that had gripped me since the night before began to desert me. I felt I was about to faint and began crying softly. Tim put his arm around me, and I clung to him.

A nurse said kindly, "Please feel free to call us anytime."

We left. Drove home. Holly hadn't nursed in almost twenty-four hours and my breasts were painfully engorged. I ran a hot bath and sat in the tub with a steaming towel draped over my breasts. Milk gushed out, relieving the pain in my breasts but not in my heart.

The next day when Tim and I went to visit Holly, a resident physician was at her bedside with his stethoscope, listening to her little body sounds. He wore a white lab coat and had wild, wavy, longish hair.

Turning to us, he said, "Don't expect this child to do as well as your other daughter."

My reaction was to blink and go numb again. Somewhere deep inside I did not believe him.

Tim told me later, "I wanted to punch his lights out."

Tim went back to work. It became my daily routine to take care of Heather's needs in the morning, then have a babysitter come and stay with her while I visited Holly. Putting on a hospital gown, I entered the ICU and sat in a rocking chair next to her crib. A nurse took her carefully from the bed, still connected to machines and tubes, and placed her in my arms. For an hour every day, I rocked her, prayed, and softly sang to her. Then I went back home to Heather. We had lunch, she had a nap, then we walked to a nearby park when the weather was good. When it wasn't, we played *Candyland,* fun for my four-year-old but certainly one of the most boring games ever for adults. We read books, and she drew or designed costumes out of my scarves and danced and laughed. Heather's laugh was so joyous, it seemed the air around her twinkled with tiny lights.

I noticed that Tim was working later and later many days. He began to sleep a lot on weekends. I didn't know then that these were signs of depression. I resented his behavior and began to lose my temper when he wouldn't get out of bed on Saturday mornings.

For two months I visited Holly every day. One day especially stands out in my mind. I walked into the ICU with the hospital gown covering my clothes. She was asleep, I thought. She was on her side with her back to me. I began to sing our special little song, one I'd made up for our hospital visits. She blinked awake and turned her head toward me. A smile broke out on her precious face when she saw me. That was a moment that I'll treasure into eternity.

The phone rang at home one day. It was the pediatric surgeon. "I'm going to close the ileostomy today. She's tolerating her feedings well, and I think this will be successful and that her bowels will now move normally."

A little relief washed over me.

Just a few days later, after my daily visit to the hospital, I was in the kitchen deciding what to fix for dinner. A nurse called with surprising news. "You can come pick up your baby now. She's discharged."

"Really?" I almost hyperventilated. "I'll be right there!"

What joy I felt! For two months, everyone but I had expected her to die. Tim even contacted his brother about a spot for her in the family cemetery in North Carolina. He only told me after she came home.

Holly was four months old. She'd been away from us and hooked up to tubes and machines for half of her life. I brought her home. Her belly had scars that looked like railroad tracks and a bandaged surgical wound that needed care, but the four of us were together again.

I longed so for a typical life for the children. It was September when Holly came home from her long visit to the ICU. We enrolled Heather in a half-day kindergarten at a nearby Presbyterian church. I carpooled with other mommies to the school, and we took our children to the park in the afternoon when the weather permitted. Holly began quarterly visits to the CF clinic where the physician was still telling me that Heather was doing well. Twice more during her first year of life, Holly was hospitalized—both times for pneumonia. After her first birthday, though, seven years passed before she was hospitalized again.

We continued going to services at the Unity Church, and I took night classes in Unity teachings offered at the church's new facility in Virginia Beach. Since I couldn't read the Old or the New Testaments without sensing too many contradictions, Unity's symbolic interpretation clicked with me. I contrasted the assurance in Psalm 8 that God made humans "a little lower than the angels and crowned them with glory and honor," with Psalm 22 in which the psalmist calls himself "a worm and not a man." Unity emphasized angel/humanity over worm/humanity and taught the closeness of humankind to the Divinity. Charles and Myrtle Fillmore founded Unity School of Christianity in 1891 after prayer healed Mrs. Fillmore of her tuberculosis, which had not responded to medical intervention. Obviously, healing for my daughters was of primary concern to me.

The doctrine, the healing, the positive slant all appealed to me.

Every afternoon while the girls napped, I had a time of affirmative prayer and meditation. Affirmative prayer focuses on a positive outcome, rather than the illness that one is observing. It requires traveling in one's imagination to a higher place and affirming that healing is taking place, rather than pleading with God to confer a miracle. Metaphysical believers consider that what we call miracles occur more often than we know in our limited human perspective.

Unity people seemed so happy and optimistic. Our Unity Church planned to have a christening ceremony one Sunday morning, and Holly was to be included. A scheduling conflict arose when Tim had to go out of town in connection with his job. I told the Unity minister of our change in plans, and her response was most certainly un-Unity-like, I thought.

"Well, I don't know what he thinks this is!" she snapped at me. "We've already ordered the flowers for the christening."

"Oh. We'll pay you for the flowers," I said, and hung up.

That was the first crack in my attraction to the Unity Church. Nevertheless, I continued my affiliation. When Tim and I were house hunting shortly after that, our Realtor took us to a pretty white house with blue shutters on a half-acre corner lot in a quiet Norfolk neighborhood. A magnificent white ash tree stretched up and over the backyard, which contained a bed of lily-of-the-valley and a small greenhouse. Just across a narrow lane from the backyard was a little park. It seemed as pastoral a setting as we could find within the city. The outside of the house enchanted us, and when we went in, we saw that the owner had a Unity Hymnal in her piano's music rack. I was sold!

The children were six-and-a-half and two years old when we moved to that sweet house. It was a pleasant June evening, our first night there, and the windows were open. The next morning, Heather climbed out of bed, her skinny arms and legs poking from a light summer nightie.

"Mommy, I woke up in the dark part of the morning, and every bird in the world was singing."

I smiled and hugged her. I loved her description of the concert that the birds performed in the trees around our house. But I wanted her to get all the sleep she needed.

"Did you go back to sleep?"

"Nope. Been lying in my bed awake ever since. I'm so sleepy."

Bittersweet—like life, like our lives in the white house with the blue doors and shutters.

~

Chrysler Hall had been open for three years and no longer needed an internal promoter, since the touring shows came with their own publicity. Tim transferred to a newly formed department at Norfolk City Hall called the Department of Marketing, Information, and Research. His title was Cultural Affairs Coordinator, and he was the city's liaison with the Chrysler Museum, MacArthur Memorial, and Scope—three big art venues in Norfolk.

Essentially, he was able to create his own job description, and he soon visualized the enormous potential that Norfolk Harbor had as a tourist attraction. His ideas caught the interest of a small group of businessmen, and together they began the campaign to transform rat-infested docks and broken-down warehouses into the area that eventually became Town Point Park. Situated on Norfolk's Elizabeth River, this tranquil spot is now the setting for festivals produced by FestEvents or merely for enjoying nature in an urban environment.

Preparations were underway nationwide for the country's 1976 bicentennial celebration that would include

Operation Sail, an international gathering of tall-masted sailing ships. Tim wanted to invite the ships to Norfolk, but he was told by a contingent of local bicentennial planners that it was "pie in the sky" to think these grand ships would come to Norfolk. However, he turned on his charm and lured several of the ships to the Norfolk Harbor for a weekend that was the precursor to the city's now well-established Harborfest. A year later, when our family got a small wooden sailboat, we named her Pie-in-the-Sky.

Tim's job developed into one requiring him to wine and dine local, national, and international visitors. John Warner, later elected to the senate from Virginia, was then the director of the American Revolution Bicentennial Administration. He was married at the time to Elizabeth Taylor. One afternoon, Tim had to attend a meeting in Williamsburg, across the James River from Norfolk. The meeting evolved into an impromptu dinner. While Tim dined with John Warner, Liz Taylor, and Virginia's Governor Mills Godwin, I was at a PTA fundraising spaghetti dinner at the elementary school where Heather was in second grade. Honestly, I didn't mind my role as Suzy Homemaker to his more glamorous public persona. But the contrast in our activities that evening seemed to me particularly ironic.

And although I certainly was, if I wanted to be, included in the social events he attended, I began to notice that his drinking at these occasions went beyond what I considered to be acceptable social drinking. Not so much that he drank too much at the functions, but that he kept right on drinking after we got home. Again it concerned me, and again I pushed my concern away.

About that time, Heather had her first hospitalization related to cystic fibrosis. She was seven. A new pediatrician had come to town and taken over the CF Clinic at King's Daughters. He was a pediatric infectious disease specialist with a keen interest in cystic fibrosis, and he became our daughters' physician for many years.

He was extremely good looking, with a Spanish accent that was sometimes hard to understand but added to his charisma; we'll call him Dr. Spain in this story. He was also brilliant and devoted to his profession. Over the years that he cared for our daughters—about twenty—he became a significant person to our entire family, and we all came to love him.

Heather was coughing and had little appetite on the day of one of her clinic visits. Dr. Spain showed me the congestion in her lungs on x-ray films.

He was later to tell me, "Her lungs looked horrible the first time I saw them."

Perhaps he didn't think I could handle such news on our initial visit with him.

She was admitted as an inpatient at CHKD for the first of what would be many, many hospital stays. Dr. Spain called these "tune-ups." Each time she was given antibiotics intravenously for a period generally lasting two to three weeks.

This meant needles in her arms attached to tubing through which the medication was administered.

Holly, on the other hand, seemed to be a thriving little girl. She had a voracious appetite, curly blonde hair, and lots of energy. At three years old, she was shaped like a pumpkin. Dr. Spain told us it was very important that she get regular CPT. Sometimes our den sounded like an orchestra's percussion section, with Tim banging on one little girl and me on the other.

Still, we continued to believe our daughters were entitled

to lives as normal as we could possibly make them. We were not overprotective. They lived their lives as fully as they were able.

Life was good, in spite of cystic fibrosis. On weekends, all four of us picnicked at Norfolk Botanical Gardens or took Sunday afternoon rides to Sandbridge, a nearby beach where we waded in the shallow surf. We vacationed at a beach house in Emerald Isle, North Carolina, owned by Tim's brother, Don. Vividly I remember the girls playing on the beach in their matching bathing suits. The suits were orange, yellow, and pink stripes with ruffles around the top. Heather at eight years old was so very thin, while Holly remained a round little muffin of a four-year-old.

Emerald Isle is across Bogue Sound from Tim's hometown. One day Tim's sister, who still lived in the same village where they grew up, took Heather over to visit with her cousins. When Holly, Tim, and I drove over in the afternoon to pick her up, she was seated on her cousin's horse, Scarlett, looking proud and joyous. It was the beginning of a love affair.

We soon discovered that both of the girls loved horses. That fall we let Heather take horseback riding lessons at Triple R Ranch. Holly was too young for lessons at the ranch, but whenever we visited Broad Creek, both girls rode their cousins' horses.

Snapshots from those times show happy little girls and cheerful parents.

Around that time, my father suffered a severe stroke and was hospitalized. I flew to Orange County, California, to be with Mom and my two sisters. Tim stayed with the girls. We spoke on the phone every day.

During one conversation, Heather announced, "Mommy,

you have to come home right away. Daddy tried to make macaroni and cheese, and he took the noodles out of the water while they were still hard. Then he got mad when the cats ate the tuna."

Tim told me later that he had stopped going to work for a few days. It was easier to try to manage things himself than to arrange for babysitters and keep up with CPT and the other necessities of our household.

I said, "Were you worried you would lose your job?"

"No. I was worried I'd lose my mind."

Dad survived, I came home, and life went on. Heather was hospitalized more and more frequently. Holly remained in good shape and developed strong little legs from constantly skating, riding her bike, and climbing trees in our yard. She sat in the tulip tree and sang like an angel. Heather jumped rope when she was well and rode her bike. When she was feeling too frail to go outside, she painted, drew, and read lots and lots of books.

Whenever Heather was hospitalized, we notified family members, as well as our Unity minister, the same one who'd gotten mad about the christening flowers. One of Tim's sisters always asked her minister to visit us, even though we did not need his services. Not only would this minister come to visit, but also ladies from his church whom we had never met came to pray and cry. It was well-meant but terribly intrusive.

Heather asked me, "Mommy, why do they always cry? Do they think I'm dying?"

She did enjoy the cards that another aunt's Sunday School class sent her, however.

Holly entered kindergarten the year Heather went to fifth grade. Heather was extremely thin and wore three pairs of socks to school to make her legs look larger. She had already been placed in programs for academically and artistically gifted students. One day, Holly's teacher called to tell me he was assigning her to a first grade class for reading. She was too advanced for the kindergarten reading program. Later she went into a program for gifted students, too. I was proud of my daughters' academic achievements.

When Heather was ten and in fifth grade, she developed severe pain in her chest late one night. The next morning, after seeing Holly off to school, I took Heather to the hospital. Heather was so weak and in so much pain that I carried her into the building in my arms. The receptionist, a dear lady, brought us a wheelchair. I wheeled her to see Dr. Spain, who immediately admitted her. X-rays revealed a pneumothorax (collapsed lung) and a pediatric surgeon was called in.

The pediatric surgeon who had performed Holly's surgeries six years previously was semi-retired by then. His own teenaged daughter had been diagnosed with Hodgkin's disease, and she'd died when my girls were nine and five. It struck me then as a ruthless irony that a man whose professional life had been devoted to helping other children would lose his own daughter to a terrible disease.

The surgeon who helped us this time was a short man with an accent that sounded British but that I later found out was South African. Heather was not handling the situation well. As the surgeon treated her in the infectious disease unit of CHKD, preparing her for a chest tube, she became very upset, almost hysterical.

"Why are you doing this to me?" she cried.

Gently, he calmed her, "I have little girls at home, and I understand you don't like this. But we have to do it."

He made a small incision through the skin and muscle, into the pleural area between the chest wall and the lungs. Tubing was inserted into the incision and then sutured into place. The tube evacuated air that had escaped from the collapsed lung and was causing pressure on the heart. Every part of it was painful and traumatic for Heather.

Traumatic for me, too. I was terrified. I talked to the Unity minister and didn't receive much compassion. She told me to visualize God's Life within Heather's body. A bit of an abstract suggestion, I think.

Dr. Spain told me, "She's just ten. She's not going to be cured."

A mist of numbness surrounded me and saved my sanity.

This was during the brief period of time at CHKD when cystic fibrosis patients were confined to the Infectious Disease Unit. It was an isolated unit, and the children were unable to leave for any reason until they were discharged. Parents and other visitors (no more than two at a time) were required to gown up for entry. That unit only lasted for a little while in the hospital, as I recall, before it was deemed to be less than ideal for the patients. Much better for the kids to be able to move about the unit, pushing IV poles, going to the playroom, or even downstairs to the snack bar when accompanied by parents. The less restrictive atmosphere made for happier patients and happier parents, and the treatments were as effective if not more so than in the depressing IDU.

I recall the wonderful adolescent unit in the second version of Children's Hospital, remodeled and expanded in 1979. Cystic fibrosis patients were admitted to this unit beginning at seven or eight, because the nurses there were so skilled in dealing with CF. The atmosphere could almost seem like summer camp. Children playing together, kids at the nurses' station twirling around in the nurses' desk chairs—generally being children, albeit afflicted children. They needed that camaraderie, the feeling that this was almost a second home and not merely a sterile clinical environment.

Of course, it was not summer camp. It was a hospital where children were stuck with needles, endured indignities to their little bodies, suffered, and sometimes died.

One day, I sat on Heather's hospital bed in the adolescent unit (AU) of the Children's Hospital of the King's Daughters. We were in the room at the end of the hall. Her arm was punctured with a needle through which fierce antibiotic medication infused and invaded her bloodstream.

My firstborn daughter said to me that day, "Mommy, I'm going to die soon. What do you think it will be like to be dead?"

She looked at me with her clear blue eyes wide and honest. My heart skipped several beats, and I began deep breathing to remain composed. This was a sacred conversation, a holy moment.

Calmly (as if I knew just what I was talking about), I responded, "You will be with God. It will be peaceful, and there will be no pain."

How could I have known to tell her there is peace after the death of the body? Perhaps we carry knowledge with us from some font of ancient wisdom, accumulated as we spiral toward our true state, nearer and nearer to God. Was there something wrong with me that I could be so composed? I was anesthetized with numbness and disbelief. A little bit of denial, of belief that my children would be healed of cystic fibrosis, kept me from alcoholism, psychotic depression, and suicide. A touch of denial can be healthy or, at the very least, a survival mechanism.

During another hospitalization, Heather suffered a second pneumothorax late one night. That night, I lay in bed next to Tim, both of us in a deep sleep. Sometime after midnight, the telephone jangled me awake. It was the head nurse on the AU.

"Mrs. Jones, Heather has had a sudden onset of severe chest pain."

My mind lurched, struggled to become fully alert. Then I heard Heather in the background, "Don't call my mother. Let her sleep."

We were all protective of one another during these lifetimes of chronic crises.

"Your mother wants to know about this," I heard the nurse say.

Into the phone she said, "She may have a collapsed lung."

After pulling on jeans and a tee shirt, I drove the dark streets from our Norfolk home to Children's Hospital. Except in the ICU, where day and night hardly vary, the hospital is a different, quieter place in the middle of the night. There are no meal trays being delivered or picked up, no housekeeping staff shampooing carpets or vacuuming. There are no clumps of earnest interns huddled in the hallways learning their profession through Socratic dialogue with the older doctors. Nurses who bustle and dart during the daytime seem to waft in and out of rooms like phantoms in the night, attending to IVs, silently taking vital signs. Heather was at the end of the hall, in the same room where she told me she would die soon.

A huge portable x-ray machine was pushed into the

room by a grumbling technician who seemed to resent being up and about at three in the morning.

The x-ray indeed revealed another pneumothorax, which would necessitate the insertion of yet another chest tube into a space between Heather's ribs and into the delicate pleura, a thin two-layered membrane that protects and cushions the lungs. The procedure had been unpleasant for her before, and she was not happy.

Six o'clock the next morning found us in the ICU, where a surgical nurse had placed a chest tube on the narrow bed. Heather's frustration boiled over. Angrily she snatched the chest tube and threw it on the floor. My job was to try and comfort her, as best I could, while my entire being ached. A chest tube was inserted as scheduled, despite one having been thrown on the floor, and Heather was in the ICU for the rest of the day.

Instinctively, I had developed a steely hard core to withstand the onslaughts of pain I experienced vicariously as my beloved daughters suffered assaults to their small bodies. And each time I left the hospital, I felt as if I carried a load of bricks on my head. I was weighted down with responsibilities, with heartache, and with barely submerged fear.

At home in time to meet Holly's school bus, I was utterly exhausted. Holly and I lay down on my bed, and I explained what had happened and asked her to understand that Mommy needed a nap before supper.

"That's okay, Mom," she chirped as she hopped out of bed, giving me a kiss on the cheek. She smelled like an elementary school. Chalk, crayons, and the sweat of recess, with overtones of last night's bubble bath and the peanut butter she'd eaten for lunch. An endearing aroma, I thought.

~

I talked to my Unity minister about my despair. Her voice was harsh with impatience as she scolded me, "Terry, you've known this would happen. This is no time to be emotional."

Her lack of empathy stunned me in spite of the forewarnings I'd had from her. I was faced with the likelihood of enduring that most aberrant of losses, the loss of my child, a loss so unnatural there is no word for it. One can be called an orphan or a widow or widower, but there is no word in the lexicon to define a bereaved parent. That conversation was the end of my association with Unity. I knew I could no longer look to that organization for comfort or inspiration. I cried and cried. I was bereft of my spiritual lifeline, or so I thought. I didn't know where to turn, but I knew I needed more humanity and far less frosty disregard of my feelings.

Later, another ex-Unity member told me that the same minister forbade her to grieve when her mother died and that she regretted not mourning. In my case, the advice was not good. Experiencing, feeling, honoring our grief is the only way to get through it and come out whole on the other side. I had needed support, not scolding.

I scoured the yellow pages for metaphysical churches, calling pastors to inquire about their theologies, finding nothing that looked or sounded appealing, I decided to try my childhood denomination again. Finding our family's spiritual framework was up to me. I drove to a service at Emmanuel Episcopal Church the following Sunday, and immediately sensed a welcoming, comforting Presence. Moreover, the Book of Common Prayer had been revised since I was last in an Episcopal church. The newer prayers were more accessible and inclusive than the long Elizabethan prayers I remember from childhood when Episcopalians were humorously referred to as God's Frozen Chosen. Kneeling for those ancient long prayers that focused on individual sin, my pre-teenaged head had spun, and I'd felt as if I would faint. In the new liturgy, there was less *mea culpa* and more inclusive loving kindness.

~

Heather's collapsed lung gradually healed, the chest tube was removed, and she came home. We were four together again, in our sweet Norfolk home with the blue shutters, under the arms of the white ash tree.

During the summer before Heather's seventh grade, she was enrolled in a program for gifted kids at Maury High School. Partway through the summer session, she developed shortness of breath and a fever. At supper one night, she seemed so weak. Her sister Holly, quite the imp at six and pretending innocence, said, "Are they gonna stick something in your arm, Heather?"

"Holly," I warned, giving her my stern mother look.

The next day Heather was admitted to CHKD where a needle was inserted into a vein of her thin arm for IV antibiotics.

She got out of her hospital bed and looked out the window in the direction of Maury High, less than a mile away. She yearned to be there. She missed her classes, her friends, and her art project. Along with another student, she was designing a three-dimensional rainbow. It was part of a dramatic scenario involving a little puppet that was supposed to walk over the rainbow and then come back to report on what was on the other side. It kept slipping off, so they put suction cups on the little figure's feet.

Released from the hospital and back home after a three-week tune-up, she ransacked her bedroom, tore things off bookshelves, and threw bric-a-brac on the purple carpet. "I know I'm just gonna go right back to the hospital!" she yelled.

Her father and I said nothing. We looked at each other, understood her frustration, and allowed the outburst to run its course. Our sadness was mingled with a tinge of amusement.

After a while, she picked everything up.

Anger is part of the whole package of chronic illness, for the patient and for the family. Anger manifests in many ways. I'm no psychiatrist, but my reading and research have taught me that when anger goes underground, it can manifest in a variety of ways, such as depression, nightmares, insomnia, fatigue, substance abuse, excessive irritability over trifling matters, and being overly polite. Or the ransacking of bedrooms.

Heather's snit was most likely as healthy as any other way she could have demonstrated anger at what life had given her.

CHAPTER FOUR

The Dead of Winter

A sad tale's best for winter.

—*The Winter's Tale,* act 2, scene 1

Now to the first dying. Dying is the word I intend, not death, because the living and the dying take place simultaneously. Somewhere deep in my heart, I've always known that death of the body is not death but a decision the soul and body make to transition to a different dimension. Isn't that part of the message of the resurrection of Jesus?

One evening when Heather was eleven and ill, she sat in the den so still, wearing a white chenille robe I'd made her. She was like an alabaster statue. I realized she didn't have the energy to move. Our seven year old was racing around the house playing a game with Tinker, our beagle. The house was arranged so that they could run a circle from the kitchen, into the den, through the living room, and back into the kitchen. When Holly touched the refrigerator she yelled, "Base!" Then both she and the dog came to a screeching halt. This game was hilarious to Holly. The contrast between the two girls that evening was startling.

Tim said to me later, in the whispered intimacy of our bed, "I believe Heather's days are numbered."

I don't think I responded. It was my turn for denial.

When she sat so still in the den, she used to say, "Mommy, come sit by me."

Usually I did. But sometimes I was too busy—so I thought then—with housework or cooking.

~

Shortly after she entered junior high school, after the interrupted summer school session at Maury High, she told me, "Mommy, I am going to die this year."

I don't remember responding. How could I?

I tried to visualize her as a young woman in her wedding dress, a skinny bride with bright blue eyes, long auburn hair, with a groom who loved her and understood her medical condition.

Maybe in a few years, a young medical student at the hospital will fall in love with her and take good care of her forever! Maybe! I fantasized.

Creative visualization is a technique using mental imagery to affect the outcome of life situations. I learned it when I was studying Unity and other New Thought philosophies, and from my days on the stage. I know it can work sometimes. Yet I was unable to creatively imagine Heather's wedding day. What I know now is that we have no influence over another's soul decisions. Even then, I think I knew deep in my heart that she would not grow up, not get married to a medical student or anyone else.

We celebrated her twelfth birthday on November 16, 1981. We feasted on her choice of menu—London broil and mashed potatoes—and then she blew out twelve candles on a chocolate cake. The candles were placed close together, so not too much breath was needed to blow them all out. Snapshots taken that day show a bone-thin girl with dark circles under happy blue eyes.

During a December visit to the doctor, he asked me what she'd been coughing up.

"Green stuff speckled with red blood," I informed him sarcastically. "Merry Christmas."

Six months after the Maury High School summer session was interrupted for a hospital tune-up and six weeks after her birthday celebration, we were in North Carolina for the New Year's holiday in Tim's hometown just west of Morehead City.

On New Year's Day, Heather seemed fairly well and was happy. We all sat down to steaming bowls of Aunt Lucy's scrumptious ham-laden black-eyed peas. Heather relished them, eating more of the traditional southern good-luck dish than the miniscule meals she usually managed. Thankfully, there are portraits of my children taken by a family photographer on January 1.

A winter storm blew in shortly after the New Year, and snow was left on the ground. A common cold could precipitate a crisis in our household. This time, both girls contracted the same infection. Holly responded to oral medication; she was getting well. The bug hit Heather harder; she was toppled by its fierce attack. She ended up hospitalized in the adolescent unit of CHKD. Her condition worsened.

After a long, slow lifetime of her body's deterioration,

she was dying. She could no longer lie down to sleep but had to spend all night with her head pressed against her hospital bed table. She was scarcely able to breathe in that uncomfortable position, but breathing was almost impossible lying down. Better to rest a little propped up, she clearly realized, than lie back and strangle.

During those last days, Heather's coughing dislodged thick, dark, mahogany-colored globs from her lungs. A hideous, poisonous substance that had no business being in the lungs of any living creature was choking our daughter to death. She was hooked up to life-prolonging oxygen, and she hated the oxygen mask that covered most of her delicate heart-shaped face. Big blue eyes looked over that mask, wide with fear and pain.

Guilt, anger, frustration, and helplessness swirled through me.

Why? I screamed to myself, when a technician poked her frail ankle for an arterial blood gas reading. *Why cause her any more pain when you can see she's dying?!*

I spoke to Dr. Spain about what I considered to be the unnecessary pain inflicted on Heather's fragile body.

"The technician has been certified and recertified," he said. His eyes were kind. "We need to determine gas exchange levels in her blood."

Maybe it was necessary and maybe it wasn't, at that stage of her life.

Holly needed a refill of her antibiotics at home. I had to leave the hospital to tend to her.

"I'll be back as soon as I can," I told Heather.

"Mommy, I hope Holly doesn't have to start coming to the hospital. I don't want her to go through all this. It's awful."

My heart cracked with love and sorrow.

I hugged my beautiful daughter as best I could around medical equipment going into her every which way. She smelled of talcum powder, hospital antiseptic, and especially pseudomonas, the nasty bacteria that infected her lungs and gave out the stench of sour fruit.

Snow began to fall as I drove away from the hospital and down the Interstate. The highway was slippery, and my mind was fogged in. My car slid. Rush hour traffic was in full swing. Drivers sounded their horns. Hardly aware of driving, I knew my firstborn daughter was dying, and I prayed, "Please, please, don't let her suffer any more!"

Snow fell from the gray sky. Tears fell from my eyes. The car was barely under my control. How did I manage to drive to the pharmacy near our home, and then to pick up Holly from a friend's home? How did I arrange for her care? Somehow those details worked out. I returned to the hospital and did not leave again while Heather lived.

"Mommy, I can't breathe!" gasped Heather when I walked into her room that evening.

I was helpless to help my child. Quickly, I closed my eyes and breathed. Breathed down to the base of my lungs; breathed all the way down to my toes. Breathed in the cleansing breath of the Spirit. Breathed out the dark heaviness weighing upon my heart.

The next day was dreary outside and inside the hospital. Dr. Spain, the girls' physician for five or six years by then, suggested we do a bronchial lavage. "Under general anesthesia, the surgeon will wash out her lungs. We can see if that will help."

It was January 18, 1982.

"Do you want to call your husband?" Dr. Spain asked me.

A moment's hesitation, and I decided. "No. Do the surgery."

Tim was in bed, without the energy to get up and get dressed, ensnared in the first of what would become many major depressive episodes. I lacked the psychological wherewithal to understand depression. It was all I could do to understand cystic fibrosis. I remained calm; I told Heather the plan.

"They're going to do a little operation to clean the gunk out of your lungs so you can breathe better."

"Can I have lunch first?"

"No, Sweetie. Nothing to eat right now."

A nurse removed her toenail polish to facilitate cyanosis evaluation during the procedure. (Cyanosis is a bluish coloration that shows up in nail beds when oxygen saturation is too low.) She was prepared for surgery. Then I called Tim. I was angry and told him that I needed him at the hospital. I needed him to get out of bed and share this crisis with me. I also called his sisters.

Hospital attendants wheeled Heather on a gurney into the elevator, down to the second floor of Children's Hospital, through the tunnel that connected King's Daughters to Norfolk General, and into the operating room. A waiting-room vigil began. In a last ditch effort to save her waning life, I had agreed to the bronchial lavage. A controversial procedure, but our only hope.

Violet, Gwen, and Grover, Tim's sisters and brother-in-law, joined me in the drab waiting room. Then Tim came. As we sat together, I heard the paging system calling Heather's resident physician. Immediately, I knew we'd lost her. But I said nothing.

Shortly, Dr. Spain entered the room. Tim and I were

holding hands. Dr. Spain glanced at our intertwined fingers and nodded.

I said, "She's gone, isn't she?"

"Yes."

Tim's head dropped backward on his neck, and he moaned, "Oh, God, no!"

"I want to see her," I pleaded.

"Oh yes, we need to see her," echoed Tim.

"Wait a minute," Dr. Spain answered, and scooted out.

Stupefied and numb, we waited as Heather was prepared for our goodbyes. We were taken to a little room where she lay pale, beginning to turn cold, and with bruises around her pretty mouth where surgical instruments had been inserted to probe her damaged lungs.

I caressed her cheek, kissed her ever so gently, whispered, "Isn't she beautiful?"

"Our little Mona Lisa," murmured her Aunt Vi.

It was then that I saw a silver cord leave Heather's body and float up toward the ceiling, where it hovered for a moment and vanished. It didn't seem strange to me, and it didn't occur to me to mention it to the others in the room.

I thought, *Her soul is leaving her body.*

Then the group of us walked toward the elevator for our final trip to Room 502. A woman who for years had been the nurse coordinator for the cystic fibrosis clinic stood by the elevator. She nodded sadly as we approached. Word had gone out through the hospital where Heather had so often spent weeks at a time. Upstairs, I hugged the nurses one by one and thanked them for taking care of her. Yet I felt wooden, as in Emily Dickinson's poem "After Great Pain": "The feet mechanical go round a wooden way." Having the sense to know that I couldn't drive, I handed my car keys over to Grover. We left the snowy parking lot in Tim's Volkswagen van.

Our priest from Emmanuel Episcopal Church met us at the house.

Although I was deadened with shock and dulled to all going on around me, an astonishing moment grabbed me. I heard Tim tell Father Michael of the silver cord that wafted from her body. He related the vision matter of factly, without embellishment or amazement. I was grateful that the phenomenon had been visible to him, too.

Later I found that the Bible refers to the silver cord in Ecclesiastes 12: 6–7: "Or ever the silver cord be loosed. . . . Then shall the dust return to the earth as it was: and the spirit shall return unto God who gave it."

Tim and I didn't discuss the silver cord. It was simply too sacred to talk about, except to acknowledge to each other that it was real.

As we lay in bed that night, Tim wept. Great gasping masculine-surrendering howls. I was quiet. Helpless. I'd never before heard a grown man cry so unabashedly. I was glad he was able to release some of his terrible grief, and I hoped I would never hear such heartrending sobs again.

After a while, maybe we slept a little.

CHAPTER FIVE

A Dog, a Horse

Why should a dog, a horse, a rat have life,
And thou no breath at all?

—*King Lear,* act 5, scene 3

On the bitterly cold January day when Heather died, our younger daughter, Holly, came home with her lips stained orange from the popsicle she was eating. She wore a purple-striped, long-sleeved tee shirt, and her hair was braided into two adorable pigtails. A friend named Katy had been taking care of her. Katy had been informed of the final outcome of Heather's ordeal, and she drove Holly home.

Katy and her family were our friends and neighbors. They had a son about Heather's age and twins, a girl and a boy, close in age to Holly. Her husband and Tim worked in the same downtown Norfolk office. Our family socialized with their family, and Holly often stayed with them after school if I was at the hospital. That snowy day, we took her into the living room, and with Father Michael's help, we told her that Heather was dead.

Her little face contorted with shock and disbelief. She sobbed. My own numbness was so overwhelming that I wonder if I comforted her enough. Many times I have asked myself if I gave her what she needed from me. Would there have been a better way to handle the telling of such traumatic news to our little girl? I do not know the answers to my questions. We did the best we could at the time, and that has to be sufficient.

Father Michael and Tim and I went to the funeral home the next day.

"Is Heather's body in this building?" I asked.

The funeral director nodded.

I shuddered.

We made funeral arrangements.

I said, "I don't like viewings."

Michael said, "You don't have to have one."

I didn't want to have a viewing, but we did. We knew it would be important to some people, to Tim's sisters. When the visitation hours were in effect, I ran in, dressed in jeans and a sweater, and left quickly. I heard Tim's brother Don say, "She's so tiny." He had a daughter born the same year, Christie, who was ten months older than Heather. An old friend from Unity Church visited, and that touched me.

Another Unity member called and remarked, "I'm sure with your spiritual understanding this is not too hard for you to get through."

Unbelievable! I was a human mother, not a saint. It was *very* hard for me to get through, and I did it the only way I knew how—one day at a time, one hour at a time, ten minutes at a time.

The service was at Emmanuel Church. The funeral limousine pulled into the parking lot and parked behind the hearse. Tim broke down. Numbness overtook me.

Tim said, "I'm so afraid of losing my composure in front of people."

"Don't be afraid, Honey. It's what people expect at funerals," I said.

Our extended families walked down the aisle, behind the casket, led by Tim and me with Holly between the two of us. She was sobbing. It was a lovely memorial service, with congregational singing of the children's hymns "All Things Bright and Beautiful" and "I Sing a Song of the Saints of God." Father Michael read the passage "On Children" from *The Prophet* and also the poem "Gone from My Sight" by Henry van Dyke. The church was full.

After the service, when friends and family came to the house, I bustled about offering cake and coffee to the guests, as if I were trying to earn the Hostess of the Year Award. Tim was in our bedroom with Jack, his best friend from university days, talking about committing suicide.

Grief is an extremely individual experience. No two people grieve exactly the same way. Anger, numbness, staying busy, feeling empty, exhaustion, nausea, insomnia, even hysterical laughter can be ways of dealing with the incomprehensible.

I stepped into the bedroom that afternoon just as Tim said, "I'll take a shotgun into the woods and have a hunting accident."

I heard but could not fathom it. He was holding a beer. He looked miserable. I went back to the mourners.

Two days later, Heather was buried in the Jones family cemetery plot in Broad Creek, North Carolina.

The next couple of years were difficult ones for us. There's a myth that most couples divorce following the death of a child. However, recent research shows that actually only 16 percent of grieving marriages end in divorce, and most of those occur within the first six months after the child's death.

Just a few days following Heather's funeral, Holly wrote,

> I loved my sister very very much
> And when she died I was very sad.
> But now she is happy where she is
> And she dose not have any pane.

Second-grade spelling, second-grade handwriting. Tearfully she told me, "Heather was teaching me to write in cursive."

Though nothing was ever the same again, our marriage survived for a combination of reasons. Lovemaking was a way we reached out to each other when we hurt too much to connect any other way. We made love a lot. Sometimes our sex was urgent and fast. Other times it was slow, luxurious, and sinuous. Sometimes it was playful. Almost always I cried afterward. The tears I shed were hot and stinging, as if the terrible accumulated pain of watching my child die poured out of my eyes like molten lava.

One night Holly came padding into our room. "Mommy, are you having a heart attack?" she asked.

"No, I'm all right."

The next morning my eight-year-old looked at me slyly and said, "I know what you and Daddy were doing last night."

The mutual love that Tim and I had for our daughters was an important link. When Holly was eight, she made a

Valentine card for me, with lots of hearts drawn on it and a message inside that read,

> I love you and Daddy very much and I hope we will all three live together for ever and ever happily ever after.
>
> Love love love love love,
>
> Holly

Finally, the connecting bond of deep love that existed at the core of our relationship held us together. We had hard times, though. Times when we groused at each other and times when we both tried to drown our sorrows in alcohol. I never drank as much as Tim did, but I drank lots of wine late at night when I couldn't sleep.

One night as I lay in bed tossing and turning, I remembered Anne Morrow Lindbergh's book *Hour of Gold, Hour of Lead.* I could hardly wait for morning to arrive, when I could dash to the local library and borrow a copy of that book. The Gold section was a bit boring, actually, all about the early days of her marriage to Charles Lindbergh. How lovely it was to eat blueberry muffins on the balcony, how handsome he was in his aviator suit.

Then—their baby was kidnapped, and the Hour of Lead began. She chronicles in her book the exact feelings and questions that I was having:

> Will everyone else die, too?
> Will we ever be safe again?
> This sharp, knife-like pain in my chest! It's a physical sensation.
> People look at me with pity and disbelief, as if I'm now another species.

I realized I needed help getting through the grief in a healthy manner. Father Michael suggested I see Dr. E, a Virginia Beach psychiatrist. I saw her for an initial appointment, and she met all my criteria as a counselor. I wanted to see a woman, one with children of her own, and one who could approach therapy from a spiritual perspective. Dr. E became for years my analyst and healer, and then my mentor, spiritual advisor, and friend. To this day, she is an important person in my life.

At my first appointment, I sobbed. "I didn't want to lose her. I wanted to keep her with me."

"I'm sorry about your daughter," she said. And she touched my shoulder as I left her office after that first meeting.

During my sessions with Dr. E, I learned a lot about myself. I wanted so much to accept our situation and the tragedy that had befallen us, and put it behind us and move onward to happiness. In some ways during those days, I lived a life of unreality in which I attempted to control everything and everyone around me. As I learned to let go of my need for control, new avenues opened. I was accepted into a master's program at a local university, and that was the start of a new career. I attended night classes. In two years, I had an advanced degree in special education, a new field for me.

~

The years passed. Holly learned to write in cursive. She grew from a little girl to a teenager to a young woman. And all the while, as she lived her life as fully as possible, her health continued to deteriorate. My mission became the sustaining of her health and her life. Our daily routine included several rounds of chest physical therapy—pounding on our daughter to clear her lungs of the stubborn buildup of thick gunk that threatened to choke her as it had done to her sister.

I realize now just how blessed I was that my children were cooperative in their treatment. I know there were many times they didn't want to adhere to the schedule and submit to the therapy, yet they did not protest too much. My eyes mist and a lump comes into my throat, thinking about a child's life in which pounding is as routine as brushing teeth.

The girls' lack of defiance toward CPT came from several sources, I believe. First, they were intelligent children and knew this therapy was necessary to maintain maximum well-being, given their conditions. Second, we made the time less boring by watching videos while we pounded, vibrated, and drained. And third, we compensated by not restricting their activities too much when they were in relatively good health. In fact, we encouraged them to participate in as much of life as they could.

I signed my first teaching contract the year Holly went to fourth grade. She attended St. Matthew's School; on Saturdays, she studied ballet at the Academy of the Tidewater Ballet. The principal at the school where I taught learning-disabled children had known Heather. He had also been principal of her elementary school and remembered our entire family. He so understood when I had to be absent from my teaching duties to take care of Holly's needs. I had a teaching assistant who was able to take over for me when I had to miss work. She and I were a good team, and I left detailed lesson plans for her whenever Holly had an appointment at the CF clinic.

It was a fortunate situation for me, because it was around that time that Holly's health began to wane. Despite all of our efforts, despite twice daily CPT, a healthy diet, and an active life, Holly's lungs began to show signs of cystic fibrosis involvement. Horrible for all three of us; this was déjà vu.

Tim and I had gotten back on the right track in our relationship. He had stopped drinking, and together we spent evenings in the hospital with Holly, coming home to a late-night supper and conversation about our lives and activities. When she wasn't hospitalized, our household was as normal as it could possibly be under the looming shadow, ever present, of cystic fibrosis.

Slowly but surely, the adolescent unit at CHKD once again became our second home. The nurses were almost like family, and I trusted them to take good care of Holly. Dr. Spain continued as primary care physician for Holly, and a social worker was available to help when we needed extra reassurance. We were grateful that Holly was never admitted to Room 502, the large room across from the nurses' station where Heather's final bed had been.

The social worker said, "That's not by accident, you know."

Professionally, life was good for me and for Tim. After teaching for a few years, I moved out of the classroom into a support staff position in a regional day program for emotionally disturbed youngsters in kindergarten through twelfth grade. My new position was instructional support teacher/counselor with the Southeastern Cooperative Educational Programs that utilized my master's level skills. I continued work with the students, which I loved doing, and mentoring their classroom teachers. Tim continued his visionary work, helping to shape the future of downtown Norfolk. Just two and a half years after Heather's death, he won the prestigious Civitan Award for Outstanding Public Service to the city of Norfolk.

Our family enjoyed happy times as we embraced the turning of the seasons together. Roller skating, bike riding, and going to Camp Holiday Trails (a camp in Charlottesville for children with chronic illnesses) during hot hazy summers gave way to anticipation of new school years, Halloween costumes, and traditional Thanksgiving dinners at Aunt Gwen's. Winter, when we were lucky, brought snow, with school closings and cold crystalline days for making snowmen and snow angels.

At a sleepover for her eleventh birthday, Holly pretended to be Olivia Newton-John as she and her pals staged an all-girl rendition of *Grease,* singing and dancing the night away.

Going through some of Heather's things, I came across a picture she'd drawn of a horse; the caption read, "I wish I could trade my bicycle for a horse."

Holly loved to ride, too. Tim and I wanted her to have a horse. So we decided to buy some land out in Suffolk, which in the '80s was still a fairly rural community with many horse farms, and build a house there. One April afternoon, Tim and I viewed a heavily wooded lot for sale on the edge of a lake. The dogwoods were blooming among the many trees, a stream ran through the property emptying into the lake, birdsong abounded, ferns and jack-in-the-pulpit covered the woodland floor. It seemed magical, enchanted, maybe even angel-filled, and we bought it.

That spring, the three quarters of our little family left alive picnicked under the dogwood trees in the sweet

Virginia woodland of our newly purchased property on Lake Prince in Suffolk.

"Our home must look as if it was dropped from the sky into a clearing just large enough for the house to fit," I told our builder.

He complied, clearing enough trees to make room for the house we'd chosen—an open, contemporary floor plan with an exterior of stone, redwood siding, and lots of glass.

Tim and I installed a large water garden in the backyard. He built a waterfall. We stocked the pond with about thirty beautiful koi and goldfish and bordered it with stone brought from a lot we'd bought on Lake Gaston.

We'd bought the Lake Gaston property while the Suffolk house was under construction.

Our banker joked, "You need a wooded lot on a lake to get away from the wooded lot on the lake where you'll be living?"

Amusing, yes, but Lake Gaston turned out to be a good investment, not only when we needed decorative rocks but later when I lived alone.

Holly's generous cousin gifted her with a horse named Mistee. It turned out that our Suffolk land, although in an area that was relatively undeveloped at the time, wasn't zoned for horses, so we boarded Mistee five minutes down the road.

Holly studied piano and ballet, and the dancing became a passion. She was photographed at the ballet studio, not in a frou-frou tutu but in workout clothes like a professional dancer in rehearsal. Black leotard, tights, pink dance skirt, and with toe shoes draped over her shoulder. Her hair in the photo, which is immortalized on the cover of an issue of King's Daughters' quarterly publication *KidStuff,* is pulled back and up in a bun in typical ballerina fashion. What's not typical about this picture are her very visible clubbed fingers.

Clubbed fingers are prevalent in individuals with cystic fibrosis. Insufficient oxygen causes the flesh under the fingernails to thicken, resulting in fingertips shaped like upside down spoons. Both my girls regarded their clubbed fingers as deformities, and each of them told me, "I'd like to chop the ends of my fingers off."

A group of medical students were making rounds one day under the guidance of a resident physician. The resident picked up Holly's hand and said, "You see how her fingers are clubbed?"

Good God, I thought, as I observed her embarrassment.

Later I suggested to Dr. Spain that perhaps some things would be better discussed away from the patient's bedside, particularly when the patient is a teenaged girl already self-conscious about her inconvenient physical condition.

He agreed. It never happened again.

~

During high school, Holly attended the Governor's Magnet School for the Arts, daily studying ballet, modern dance, and jazz. I believe the vigorous aerobic activity involved in dancing helped keep her healthier and extended her life.

"I'm gurgling," she told me at the Suffolk Courthouse when we went to get her driver's license. She meant she could hear and feel the congestion rattling around in her lungs. It meant another hospitalization was on the horizon.

Watershed events important to most children and teens—birthday parties, learner's permit, proms, SATs, driver's license—had to share time with hospital stays at CHKD for "tune-ups," courses of powerful intravenous antibiotic treatment.

Extended IV treatments were accomplished at home, under the care of a home health nurse. Home healthcare hadn't been available while Heather was living. The nurse arrived at regularly scheduled times to change a line or restart an IV, but it fell to us to make sure the medications were hung on the IV pole at prescribed times, usually every four hours for an hour at a time. Our sleep patterns reverted to the days of the children's infancies, when we woke up every few hours for feedings. It was well worth the loss of sleep to have our daughter at home with us.

When Holly was in high school, her assistant principal arranged for the Suffolk School Board to grant her "as needed" homebound status. She could attend school when she was well enough and obtain homebound instruction without having to go through red tape each and every time it became necessary. The librarian at Nansemond River High School became her homebound teacher, helping her to keep up with her peers.

Still, she maintained a normal young girl's life as much as possible. The mayor of Norfolk sponsored her as an attendant to the Italian princess in the annual Azalea Festival, which later became the Norfolk NATO Festival. This was quite an honor for our seventeen-year-old daughter. She was fitted for her pink satin gown with a heparin-locked IV site wrapped in gauze on her forearm. We went to the fitting between drug infusions. The seamstress was polite enough not to inquire, though I'm sure she was curious about the bandaged arm. Fortunately, the course of medication was completed before the festival began, and

Holly rode in the parade and attended the festival ball on the arm of her VMI escort with no outward trappings of cystic fibrosis.

On the first day of her senior year, she was late to English class and there were no seats left. One of the boys, Scott, got up and offered her his seat. She accepted.

He told me later, "She was so cute! Those blue eyes and blonde hair, and breathing heavily. I thought that was from dashing into class late. Wow! She was a real looker."

They started dating and became steadies for the rest of the school year. In August, they went away to college, Scott to William and Mary and Holly to Longwood.

For three weeks she lived valiantly as a college coed in her dorm in Farmville. Just three weeks. She made the choice to return home, ill and disappointed, realizing she could not survive away. She needed the care-giving that her dad and I provided.

When she came home from college, Holly was so sick that she had to be hospitalized. She sat on a gurney in an outpatient exam room and, plain and simple, told Dr. Spain, "I overdid it."

What college freshman doesn't overdo it? What college freshman doesn't want to stay up half the night eating pizza with her dorm mates?

He smiled ruefully and admitted her.

After her body revived a bit, after her mind and spirit accepted that she would not return to dorm and college life, she settled herself into a routine here at home. She had lost a lot of weight. She was getting very thin, just like Heather. We made sure that she had plenty of good quality, high-calorie meals and snacks.

~

The tiny church in the Chuckatuck section of Suffolk where we'd transferred our membership from Emmanuel was publishing a new directory. Olan Mills Studio would be at the church to take members' portraits. Our priest, knowing Holly had spare time, asked her to be the registrar during the two days of photographing

"Sure, I'll do it," she agreed.

On the first day of photography sessions, a strange little scruffy brown dog attached itself to Holly and jumped into her car when she opened the door. It was love at first sight between the spunky young lady and the lost (or abandoned) and uncollared dog. Immediately, Holly christened her dog "Sugar."

"She's the sweetest little dog I've ever seen. She's my Sugar!"

But when she arrived home with the straggly creature, Tim said, "We know nothing of this dog's history or origins. We simply can't keep her."

At that time, he was breeding and training pedigreed Brittanies, and we already had three of those beautiful and energetic dogs.

Holly was crestfallen. "Why? She won't bother the Brittanies."

"Just won't work," said her dad.

"I have an idea," I said. "Since you're footloose these days, let's take Sugar back to the churchyard and set up food, water, and a bed. You can visit her every day."

We drove back to St. John's. Holly sat in the passenger seat, tears pouring over Sugar on her lap. We arranged the bed, water, and food in a covered courtyard next to the parish hall.

The following day, Sugar was missing. The bed had been slept in, the food was eaten, but there was no Sugar. Holly ran over to the church caretaker's house next door.

"Have you seen a skinny little brown dog?" she asked.

"Yes," he replied. "But there's a pack of wild dogs threatening livestock in this area. I didn't want that dog to join the pack, so I called Animal Control, and they picked her up."

Quick as a New York minute, Holly was on the phone to Animal Control. Yes, they had a dog fitting Sugar's description. Quicker than a New York minute, Holly dashed to the pound and there was Sugar, who leapt in her cage when she saw her new friend. Holly paid the ten-dollar adoption fee and took the dog straight to the veterinarian's office for a checkup. The vet said she was a spayed female, probably about two years old, and that all she needed would be tender loving care and a nourishing diet.

Holly brought Sugar home and explained everything—the pack of wild dogs, the farmers' livestock, and the adoption procedure. Tim's heart couldn't help but melt. He gave in and welcomed the mutt into our household. He never for a moment regretted it. Sugar and Holly became inseparable.

For the spring semester of that school year, she enrolled in college at Christopher Newport University, closer to home. She commuted daily across the James River Bridge with her best friend, Stacie.

I'm so grateful for Stacie's ongoing friendship and for Scott in Holly's life! Neither of them really seemed to notice her frailty, even when she became virtually housebound. Even when she couldn't be away from an oxygen tank for longer than a few minutes. Even when her face became bloated from the high doses of prednisone she took. Stacie was still her best friend, visiting her in the hospital and talking endless hours on the phone as teenaged girls do.

And Scott was still her boyfriend, loyal beyond the capability of most young men faced with a housebound girlfriend. He gave her a promise ring, an emerald, her birthstone, flanked by little diamonds.

"For eternal love," he said.

I'm also grateful for her pets, and for the mystical bond she experienced with them. Throughout middle and high school, Holly rode her horse, Mistee, with happy abandon and spent countless hours grooming Mistee, combing her mane, picking her hooves, kissing her nose, offering openhanded gifts of carrots and apples for Mistee's big square teeth to chomp on. There were other pets, too. Out in our backyard is the grave of a gerbil whose dead body stayed in our freezer in a Ziploc bag until I convinced Holly that the poor little thing needed a proper interment.

Exactly two years after she and Sugar found each other, Holly called me at the school where I worked. Frantic! Emergency! Sugar had been hit by a car! I raced home. We located her by the side of the road and with the help of a neighbor and a blanket, got her into my car and took her to the vet. Holly squeezed her eyes closed and tightly clasped her hands in prayer while the dog was being examined in another room. The doctor came out, shaking his head. No saving Sugar. With heavy hearts, we brought Sugar's body home in a box and laid it on the kitchen floor.

I called Tim. "Please come home. There's been an emergency, and we need your help."

He arrived shortly.

Holly sat on the floor pleading with Sugar to come back

to life. She refused to eat. I heated a bowl of soup and spoon fed it to my daughter until she refused even that.

"I can't eat any more," she said.

Her tiny, frail body could scarcely withstand the missing of a meal.

"I want to have her stuffed," she wept, "and keep her forever."

But Tim dug a little grave, and we had a funeral, burying Sugar in the woods in back of the house. It was a sad, sad day. Death had visited our family again.

~

During the years following Holly's return from college, her health steadily declined. She was hospitalized more and more often.

Dr. Spain suggested implanting a Port-a-Cath into her upper chest. The embedded catheter could be accessed for IV infusion, and she could avoid the frequent needle punctures in her arm. It made good sense to Tim and me.

Holly announced, "I'm not getting that thing put in my chest. Not where it'll show when I wear a bathing suit."

She discovered that a Richmond hospital was implanting Port-a-Caths in the arm rather than the chest. She told Dr. Spain of this and that she'd agree to that procedure if he'd work it out.

Along with the Port-a-Cath, she had a G-button inserted—a gastric tube in her abdomen for nighttime feedings. She didn't object to that one. She couldn't wear two-piece bathing suits anyway, because her belly was covered in scars from her infant surgeries.

She'd been accepted into the lung transplant program at the University of Virginia Medical Center by then, and the transplant team needed her to gain weight. In addition to eating three healthy meals a day plus snacks, her G-button delivered supplementary liquid nutrition through an IV drip while she slept. For months, each night she hooked herself up to the feeding tube.

Each and every morning she got up and vomited it all out. Oh well.

By the time she was twenty, we had oxygen tanks in the house on a permanent basis. A long, long tube enabled her to move about the entire house, still connected to the oxygen tank that was in her bedroom. Without supplemental oxygen, her oxygen levels could become dangerously low.

She was by then being seen routinely at the University of Virginia instead of CHKD, since she was on the transplant list at the Charlottesville facility. One day a physician at UVA looked at her G-button, saw how raw and irritated the skin around it was, and yanked it out. No warning. Pop! The device was out.

"Ouch!" she yelled. Then she laughed. She was happy to be rid of that supposed weight-gaining device that wasn't doing its job anyway.

Holly worked very hard to stay as healthy as she could while we waited and prayed for her transplant.

But cystic fibrosis is an insidious, obstinate, and tenacious disease. In spite of constant care, frequent hospitalizations, daily treatments and medications, as well as all the prayer and love we could muster, her condition worsened, declined, deteriorated.

Occasionally we read in the newspaper about new discoveries and advances in the treatment of cystic fibrosis. Gene therapy was one of those. When we first read about it, Tim said, "Maybe we'll have grandchildren after all."

I sat and looked at him, and tried to smile. "I hope so."

Oh, how I hoped.

Tim had written a poem that's inscribed on Heather's gravestone:

Like him in whose mansion
She now resides,
She came so short a time to teach
Her tender lesson of love and light,
Returning whence she came
To His good might,
To wait for us.

To wait for *us*. For Tim and for me. Surely, much, much later for Holly. Not now though! Not now! Not while she was young, filled with life and love and a future maybe to include her children. Only twenty-two years old. Tim and I must die first.

My belief remained that God would not allow us to become bereaved parents twice in one lifetime.

The thought was absolutely too horrible, too incomprehensible.

CHAPTER SIX

No Breath at All

Look on her! look, her lips,
Look there, look there—
He dies.

—*King Lear,* act 5, scene 3

What more eloquent and mournful elegy for a dead daughter than these words uttered by Shakespeare's brokenhearted, aged, bereft, and battered monarch? He wailed and he moaned with an anguish I knew well. Then he died. King Lear died, just as I was certain I would if Holly were to be taken from us. I was certain that I could not survive the loss of a second beloved daughter. Holly grew profoundly ill, requiring oxygen at home twenty-four hours a day. She could no longer attend college or go out with her friends. Friends continued to visit her as she awaited a donor for a bilateral lung transplant.

I read about living donor lung transplantation. Human

beings have five lung lobes, three in the right lung and two in the left lung. Two donors give one lobe each, leaving each donor with four lobes. The donors donate either a left or right lower lobe each. Both of the recipient's damaged lungs would be removed, and she would receive two new lung lobes, one from each donor. I asked Dr. Spain about it.

He said, "They are doing it in California. Perhaps I could fly out to Los Angeles and inquire about the procedure. An advantage is that the living related-donor procedure could be planned in advance. But it involves a seriously invasive surgery for all three of you. Are you sure you want to consider it?"

"I am very, very sure."

Tim and I both wanted to find out more. We desperately desired to give Holly a second gift of life.

My mind and heart reverberated with the wretched keen of King Lear on the windswept moors of ancient Britain. Truly, I imagined my husband and I making a suicide pact and dying together like a middle-aged Romeo and Juliet if our second daughter were taken from us.

Holly had been hospitalized in Charlottesville for a few days. Hospitalizations at the University of Virginia Medical Center had become routine for her. She was too old for Children's Hospital. She was our child, Tim's and mine, but she had become our adult daughter. I don't recall that she ever packed up and drove herself to Charlottesville. Always one or both of us would drive up with her, but she had no problem with us leaving her there. It was a teaching hospital, and we trusted the staff to take good care of her.

She'd made friends in Charlottesville. There was another CF patient and his family whom she became close with. Some of the nurses were her age, and they hung out in her room when they could. Tim had twenty-eight nieces and nephews in his large family, and a couple of her many cousins were students at UVA. They visited.

She was twenty-two, and it was the first week of November 1996. I was at my desk on the second floor of the Southeastern Cooperative Educational Program in Suffolk's old Thomas Jefferson School when Holly called.

"Mom, they want to do another sinus surgery. They want to make sure my sinuses are clear for the transplant. I need you and Dad to come up here. I'll be in and out of the operating room in no time, but I need you here."

She sounded chipper, brave and vivacious. I called Tim at his office. We met at the house, tossed a few personal necessities into an overnight bag, jumped in the car, and scooted up the road to Charlottesville. A three-and-a-half-hour drive, a one-night stay, and we expected to be back the next day.

We arrived at the hospital. We rode the elevator up to Three West and dashed into the little anteroom that separated Holly's room from the pulmonary unit's main hallway. We robed up and then entered her room, eager to see her. Holly was perched on a gurney with a hospital attendant standing by to wheel her down to the OR. We'd arrived just in time! She looked perky and cheerful.

She glanced at Tim in his requisite protective paper hospital gown and quipped, "Hey Dad, you're stylin'!"

Her optimism amazed us, because she'd had a sinus surgery once before at CHKD a couple of years earlier. She suffered miserably during the recovery period. Yet her attitude was upbeat and positive. She was taken into the operating room, and yet again, Tim and I began another waiting room vigil. Yet again, Holly was in surgery. Yet again, a daughter of ours was under the knife.

Tim read the newspaper; I leafed through a magazine. Our waiting time grew and grew, became interminable. What's wrong? We were restless. This was taking too long. We'd received no word.

Finally, word came. Holly was having difficulty waking up from the anesthesia. They had almost lost her on the operating table.

She had pulled through, though. Finally. Barely. Unconscious and intubated, she'd been transferred to the medical intensive care unit (MICU). Stupefied, we returned to her room on Three West.

One of her favorite nurses bluntly told us, "You need to begin to visualize your life without Holly."

We stared at this well-meaning young woman in numb terror. Numb terror, helpless numb terror! No other words can describe that dreadful night. We were allowed to stay in her room until morning, I in her hospital bed and Tim in a reclining chair next to me. Prayers and supplications punctuated that night of desperate fitful sleep. I tried to pray from the bottom of my heart, and we called others for prayer support.

"Please pray for Holly. Please!" This was our heartfelt entreaty.

Prayer, I have come to believe, aligns our hearts and minds with what is good. Prayer gives us the strength to change our own attitudes and situations and to accept with grace our lives as they are given to us. At least for me, it has opened my consciousness to new ideas and insights and to ways of becoming a channel for good. Prayer does not change God, I don't believe; rather it opens our hearts to receive God's love, power, wisdom, and grace. Positive prayer helps to invoke blessings in our lives and to bestow Light upon others. I've experienced great power in the dynamic of group prayer.

I don't believe that prayer is synonymous with begging and pleading; nevertheless, my prayers became elemental, simplistic, and even infantile during those rollercoaster November nights and days in Charlottesville. I was like a child begging for a special favor.

The journal I kept was always with me. As I reread my beseeching monologue, there is no question that I had one goal, one wish, one desire, and one prayer: Holly's survival.

~

I began keeping the journal in 1974, when I was pregnant with Holly. At the time, I knew only that doing so helped me to focus, to calm down, and to get beyond my mind's monkey chatter. Journaling became addictive for me. Every morning I sat with a cup of coffee, a spiral notebook, and a pen. Shortly after I began this practice, I learned that journaling was becoming a widely used technique for healing within the therapeutic community. How-to books have since been written on the subject, with hints and strategies that various authors consider the most advantageous methods of making the most of the process.

My own journaling has evolved over thirty-plus years. With all due respect to some excellent writers who insist that journals must be handwritten for greatest effectiveness, I now find that using my word processor works better for me than the spiral notebook and pen. I'm a fast touch typist, and I can close my eyes and let my thoughts and feelings stream out through my fingertips. The process centers me and allows what needs to be released from my subconscious to come out. This daily ritual is a form of meditation and prayer that has helped save my sanity.

The entries quoted in these chapters were handwritten during our time of waiting, watching, hoping, and praying in the hospital in Charlottesville and are set apart.

7th of November 1996.

Holly survived the night, thanks be to God.

She lingered unconscious and intubated; her beautiful body punctured by an assortment of needles and tubes. Rain fell lightly outside the hospital. Holly always enjoyed the calm cleansing quality of an occasional rainy day, just like me. The wet staccato patter against the windowpanes could be mesmerizing for us both. But this rainy day she was in a windowless cubicle in the medical intensive care unit, eyes closed, machines breathing for her. I longed to hear her voice, to look into her eyes, open and alert again, to listen with her to the rain's rhythmic patter on windowpanes and roof.

The pulmonologist at UVA who coordinated her care arranged a conference concerning her status. All staff on the unit who could take time from their duties, as well as one of the hospital chaplains and the nurse coordinator for the transplant program, attended the meeting. The pulmonologist told Tim and me that most of them were there for the love of Holly, not because they were required to be by their job descriptions. We were deeply touched. They sat in a semicircle around the two of us, and we discussed the possibility and ethics of parents serving as living donors. We could each give our daughter a portion of our healthy lung lobes.

This procedure had never been done at the University of Virginia, but it had been done elsewhere. It was our intense desire to give this gift of renewed life to our daughter, and we bared our souls' hopes and longings in the conference room with the healthcare staff.

The conference ended on a hopeful note.

Then we sat and waited. Sat and waited, waited, waited. Waited. Late that morning, we met with two members of the Medical Ethics Committee concerning our plans to be living related donors. Tim and I, along with a retired surgeon and medical professor and a hospital chaplain who was very pregnant, sat together at a large table in a conference room, considering the ethical implications of the proposed three-way surgery. The hospital was ambivalent about the surgeries. The surgeons did not really want to perform this three-way procedure, which was unprecedented in Virginia at that time. They did not want to do what they had never done before.

Just before noon, I wrote a letter to God:

Dear God,

Please bring lungs to Holly. I deeply desperately pray that she will receive perfect donor lungs as quickly as possible.

Please, I am not asking You for a "miracle healing," for her diseased lungs *suddenly* to *regenerate!*

But I *am* asking You to provide perfect lungs. Please bring perfect healthy lungs to Holly for her transplant. Please.

I am asking You, Lord.

And I Thank You for always knowing our needs, and always providing. You know what we need and You are the constant provider.

Amen from your daughter,

Terry

~

Around two thirty in the afternoon I was in the MICU when Holly opened her eyes and looked at me. During this most tender of moments, I felt a profound psychic connection pass between us. Gratefully, I drank into my heart her soft eyes widening with recognition and love. The crisp and efficient MICU nurse who was standing beside me murmured in awe at the gentle intensity of this private moment. The love I shared with my daughter was palpable.

My memory took me to that time almost twenty-two years earlier when, gowned and masked in protective hospital gear, I entered the ICU. Holly was in an impersonal hospital crib with her eyes closed and her little body very still. I began to sing our special little song. Immediately her eyes opened and she looked at me, smiled, and it seemed to me she came to life.

Now, in 1996 and newly returned to consciousness, Holly was given chest physical therapy by way of a percussion vest. She received a blood transfusion to increase her hemoglobin.

After she regained consciousness, she couldn't talk because of the endotracheal intubation. A tube was inserted between her vocal chords and into her trachea to assist her breathing. She tried to write a note to us. She tried so hard, with such determination. We watched—Tim, the nurse, and I.

She couldn't write cursive, and her nurse suggested she try printing, one letter at a time. Finally, with her compromised fine motor skills hindering her efforts, she gave up in exasperation and threw the pencil on the bed. But I continued to encourage her, knowing pretty well what she was saying. I helped her hold the pencil and together we got the sentence down on paper: "This wasn't supposed to happen."

She fell back, exhausted from the effort, but I felt some relief.

She is improving! I noted in my journal.

Then the practicalities of our decision to donate lung lobes began. Tim and I were given physical exams along with x-rays and pulmonary function tests to determine our physical suitability.

A doctor asked me, "Can you walk up three flights of stairs?"

"Oh, yes!"

"When did you last do it?"

"Today. I usually use the stairs instead of the elevator to get to her room."

A resident said to the older doctor, "That's actually more than three flights." Grim nods all around.

This will work! This will happen, Tim and I believed.

We were exhausted from sleep deprivation and frantic worry, but we were hopeful and had no doubt our bodies would prove worthy of lung lobe donation.

The following day was the third after Holly's sinus surgery. The evaluation process continued for Tim and me.

A team consisting of the transplant nurse coordinator, the social worker for the transplant clinic, and a neuropsychologist interviewed Tim. It was a psychological assessment and took quite a while. Among other things, he told me that they asked him what he intended to be doing in five years.

"I'm going to put a sail on top of our van and sail across America with my wife!"

I learned that there was laughter all around the table, as the team relaxed and the meeting ended. We felt that the process was moving right along. The nurse coordinator told us to be prepared for publicity and press interviews.

But later that same day, the living donor plan was put on hold. And this was partly due to our daughter's expressed opposition. She seemed to improve. She was apprehensive about her parents putting their own lives on the line, and said so. The pulmonologist reminded us that since she was an adult, we had to respect her wishes. We understood. Nevertheless we felt thwarted. Terribly thwarted and so scared.

We stayed at the hospital until late at night and then went to a home near the university where we had a room. Early the next morning, we returned to the MICU waiting room.

Whenever we wanted to visit her, we had to phone the unit from the waiting room to ask the nurse's permission to enter.

I sat in the MICU waiting room and listened to Holly's nurse tell me over the phone that Holly had had a pretty good night. She woke up intermittently and became agitated, wanting the tubes out. The staff was doing weaning tests in preparation for extubating her. In other words, the mechanical ventilation was gradually changed to allow her to initiate more breaths on her own while the ventilator provided fewer breaths. All the while, her vital signs were closely monitored, and we couldn't see her.

By eleven that morning, Holly was extubated. Cystic fibrosis treatments and therapies have improved drastically since our daughters were living and dying. Back then, it was assumed in the CF community that once a patient was intubated, there was no going back, and the death knell was about to ring. So it would be an understatement to say we were thrilled. By five thirty that evening she was out of intensive care and back on the 3 West unit, in Room 3173.

We had lived through a nightmare. I had not joined King Lear on the windswept moor. I had no need to howl. I wrote simply:

Thank you that the nightmare is over. Amen.
Thank you for Holly. Amen.

The possibility of our living related-donor transplant had been put on the back burner. But it wasn't ruled out, so I went through a psychological evaluation with the same committee of people who had interviewed Tim. My assessment was over and done with more quickly.

I wrote:

Guess I'm not as entertaining as my husband.

Now, years later, I don't have the foggiest recall of the questions they asked or anything about the conversation. I remember the conference room and the long polished table. I remember trying to present myself as strong and upbeat. I pasted the best Power-of-Positive-Thinking look I could muster onto my face while the team members observed my every gesture and listened to every nuanced word I uttered.

I remember little about the others at the table. All I knew was that I had to convince them that I was a good candidate for donating part of my lung to my daughter.

After my psychological evaluation, we waited some more. We did so much waiting and sitting. Sitting in the waiting room. Sitting and waiting. We'd believe that soon, the next day perhaps or the day afterward, we'd be allowed to give portions of our healthy lungs to our precious daughter. We could give new life to her. Tonight? Tomorrow?

Waiting.

Holly jotted the following message to me: "When I first woke up on Sat., everything and everyone was black-n-white. I thought I had lost my vision."

"We thought we had lost you, Holly."

My heart felt as if it were bursting apart with actual physical pain.

~

In spite of our weariness, anxiety, and trepidation, I knew we had so much for which to be grateful. Holly was receiving the best available medical attention, and the staff's caring attitude toward family members was profoundly helpful. Our wide network of supportive friends and family surrounded us—literally or by phone and in prayer. Tim and I had a wonderful home away from home, a fortuitous bonus in this difficult time.

We were guests at a grand old estate just north of the hospital. A Mount Vernon style house in Keswick, it was about nine miles from the University of Virginia campus, called the grounds at UVA. "Leicester," the estate with its acreage and horse barns, belonged to a woman named Sandra, who lived there with her four children. One of her sons had cystic fibrosis. Holly had become friends with him and his sisters and brother during several hospital stays. This friendly family opened their home to us with graciousness and generosity.

They gave us an upstairs guest room where we slept in twin beds, like husband and wife in a 1950s' sitcom. The beds were lovely antiques, and the room was spacious, with a chest of drawers, a dressing table, and a nightstand between the two beds. A corner room, it had windows on two sides, with a small bathroom adjoining. We were very comfortable there. Considering the circumstances, considering that our daughter was in critical condition just down the road.

~

The evening of Tuesday, November 12, found us back in an intensive care unit, frantic with concern. Holly's fever was up and her blood pressure way down. Now Tim was irate. With no cadaver lungs available and our daughter gasping for breath, he wanted to proceed with the living donor surgeries. The physicians were dragging their feet.

Tim mentioned that he had details to take care of in Norfolk, and it would be helpful to schedule our surgeries so that he could tend to business first.

The pulmonologist responded, "We won't do this for your convenience."

It made no sense to us. Our girls' longtime physician in Norfolk, Dr. Spain, had told me several times that an advantage of the living donor surgery was that it could be done at a time convenient for the donors.

The Charlottesville physician's snappy retort infuriated Tim, but he didn't show it. Only I, who knew Tim so well, recognized his inward anger.

And Holly still resisted the living donor plan. I wanted whatever was best for her, with the stipulation that whatever was best meant getting her well again.

Early in the morning of November 13, I wrote:

> *This helpless feeling . . . nightmares (literal & waking) . . . terror . . .*
>
> *Oh Dear God I pray, send good lungs to my precious Holly one way or another. What will happen next?*

Sometimes, as I was journaling, it seemed to me that God spoke to me through my writing. I wrote/heard these words:

> *I am here for you.*
> *I am always within you.*
> *Have no doubt concerning that truth,*
> *That absolute Truth.*
> *I am in you and in Holly and*
> *That is very important for you to remember.*
> *My spirit is deep and strong in your treasure Holly.*
> *I will never ever desert you or Holly.*
> *My work is being accomplished in and through her.*
> *Let it happen.*
> *Stay quiet this day.*
> *Be at peace.*
> *Take care of self and accept the Love that surrounds you.*
> *I Will Take Care of precious Holly. I promise.*
> *Go Forth into Your Day in Peace, Promise, & expecting only Good.*
> *It will come!*

Now, far removed from 1992, I ask myself, was it God? Or was it wishful thinking? I don't think it matters. The words soothed me when I needed to be soothed, nonstandard capitalization and all.

It snowed that night in Charlottesville. In the morning, there was snow dusted like confectioner's sugar on the lawn at Leicester, and again it seemed that God spoke to me through my journal:

> *Here is what you need to know this morning: It is not your responsibility to take care of anyone else today. You don't need to and should not take Tim's sorrows, feelings, or disappointments upon yourself. You have enough to deal with shouldering your own feelings, sorrows, and disappointments. Just be who you are today. Heed advice to take care of yourself.*

Perhaps this was my own inner knowing. Or maybe a God-spark in all of us that speaks to us sometimes, which would make the inner knowing a sort of direct line from God. Whatever the source, it was good guidance and not to be ignored.

On Friday, November 15, at four p.m., Holly was once again out of the ICU and back in her own hospital room. I was sitting with her. The pulmonologist came in and announced, "We're going to do a transplant tonight."

I thought to myself, *That's nice. I wonder who?*

I don't know why I didn't quite comprehend.

Then I realized that he was talking about Holly, and exhilaration bubbled through me. Someone ran out to the waiting room to get Tim. The look of sheer joy on his face when he dashed through the doorway into Holly's room is an image that has never left me.

The news spread throughout the unit and beyond. One by one, enthusiastic staff members popped into the room.

A respiratory therapist came in and said, "Congratulations! We've all been waiting for this."

A nurse bustled in with a big smile on her face and some nail polish remover, saying, "The nail polish has to come off."

I had another flashback to 1982, when they removed Heather's bright pink toenail polish before her bronchial lavage, so that the anesthesiologist and nurses could monitor the color of the nail beds.

A physical therapist who had worked with Holly to keep her muscles from atrophying said, "Guess what, kiddo? Today's my birthday, so it can't go wrong!"

The chaplain, who was a member of the Ethics Committee, talked with Tim in the hallway and then came in the room to offer Holly prayers and good wishes.

A cardiovascular surgery resident came in, drew blood from Holly's arm, and had her sign consent forms.

Then, an attendant arrived with a stretcher. We were all three giddy with excitement. Tim and I, along with a couple of friends, walked the hospital corridors beside our only surviving daughter. She was wheeled toward the operating room where she would get her long-awaited new lungs. The attendant pushing the gurney observed to her, "You have a strong support system." We all grinned.

Suddenly she propped herself up and asked for a pencil and something to write on. I handed her a book I was reading, and she opened it to a blank page. There, recorded forever on the inside back cover of my paperback book, in shaky printing, Holly wrote this message to us:

> I have to do it now—if this is right for me. If God and Heather and Grandma are there with me, I'll be fine wherever that "place" will be.

CHAPTER SEVEN

To Dance Again

When you do dance, I wish you a wave o' the sea
that you may ever do
Nothing but that.

—*The Winter's Tale,* act 4, scene 4

We kept an all-night vigil in the family waiting room while Holly was undergoing her bilateral lung transplant. Word went out to family and friends far and near. Dr. Spain called from Norfolk to express his hope for a good outcome. Others called to offer prayers, encouragement, and good wishes.

Our precious Holly was getting her new lungs. We realized that our good fortune came at the expense of another family's tragedy. We were very grateful for their compassionate generosity, whoever they might be.

At six twenty on the morning of Saturday, November 16, her doctors told us the surgery had been successful and that she was stable.

"You'll be able to see her soon," the pulmonologist told us.

Our priest from St. John's in Suffolk walked into the waiting room. He had driven four hours from the little parish where Holly and Sugar had found each other to rejoice with us. Things seemed so right.

But abruptly our elation ended. Four hours passed. We didn't understand. The doctor had said we could see her "soon." Finally, the pulmonologist and a surgeon walked into the waiting room, shoulders slumped. They led us into a conference room where one stated bluntly, "Holly has taken a turn for the worse."

The blood in my veins suddenly felt like ice water. My head seemed to be spinning right off my body.

Holly was comatose.

"We've placed her into a drug-induced coma to prevent her possible agitation and to facilitate her healing," said one of the doctors.

We were plunged back into a nightmare again.

My memories of the next few days are vague, but I know that I prayed for Holly's recovery. Helplessly, I wondered what else I could do for my daughter whom I loved so much. One afternoon my sister Emmy called me and asked, "Do you remember what day this is?"

"No," I said.

"Oh, Terry, it's Heather's birthday."

It was—would have been—Heather's twenty-seventh birthday. Oh dear heavens. Desperate for signs and wonders, I took this as a good omen. I needed assurance that Somebody Out There was helping Holly return to us. Assurance and hope despite the fact that she was immobilized, bandaged, hooked up to life support.

On Sunday, November 17, it seemed to us that she was gradually getting stronger. We based our hopefulness on vital signs as reported by the nurses, as well as encouraging comments from hospital staff. I remember a social worker reassuring us, "She's taking little bitty baby steps."

Many visitors came to be with us, both family and friends. I told myself that everyone who came out of her little room in the Thoracic Cardiovascular Post-Op Unit (TCVPO) looked happy. I was thankful for this and certain they could see the improvement that was surely taking place.

A spiritual force was holding us up. I yearned to hear the voice of God and to see God's hand at work. The next morning, I recorded the following dream in my journal:

November 18th 11:30 a.m.

> *I had a dream so vivid. I desired Jesus with an ecstatic longing. He was with me. He was loving and compassionate but at the same time dispassionate. I knew He loved me and I had to be willing to go on a journey with Him. That's the journey I'm on! Craving Divine Union.*

At three thirty that afternoon, the pulmonologist told us, "I see no obstacles to her complete recovery." He said the plan was to remove the ECMO machine (an acronym for Extra Corporeal Membrane Oxygenation) the next morning.

The ECMO is a bypass machine that performs the work of the lungs to oxygenate the blood. Thus, the lungs themselves have nothing to do but heal. I understand that now, but the last thing on my mind at the time was any wish to know the technicalities of her treatment. I knew that the ECMO functioned on behalf of her organs, and that was enough. I did not care how it worked, nor could I have processed a scientific explanation then. I knew only that the doctor's outlook was optimistic.

I went for a walk in soothing light rain, and felt refreshed.

The next few days blended into an amorphous blob of sameness. Gone was our hope that we might give Holly portions of our lungs. Gone even was the anger we felt when our living donor status was put on hold. Gone was the euphoria we felt the night the transplant took place. The hours passed gray and lengthy. We sat in the family waiting room, and when the need to see our daughter overtook one or the other of us, we made a phone call to TCVPO and requested permission to enter.

Visitors came and went, bringing flowers for Holly and books for us. They took us to lunch and dinner.

One of the doctors commented to me, "You look like you're existing on black coffee." But always I sat like an android and nibbled when food was placed in front of me.

A friend called to tell us there was a sign in the Food Lion parking lot on Route 17 in Suffolk. The sign read:

STATE-WIDE PRAYER VIGIL
FOR
HOLLY JONES

Vaguely, I wondered who had put the sign up.

The doctors asked us to have someone coming up from home bring a picture of Holly so the hospital staff could see what she looked like before the lung transplant. Several of her cousins and her aunt brought photos, including a large framed portrait taken for her high school yearbook.

She was beautiful and vibrant in the photos, and constantly I prayed that she would come back to us just like that.

> *Please God, bring our Holly back to us with her healthy new lungs.*

Journaling and praying helped keep me afloat.

On Thursday the 21st, I woke up in the wee hours of the morning with my body aching and my eyes burning. Convinced that I was feeling pain on Holly's behalf, I vowed, *I willingly take her pain.*

I went back to sleep, and when I woke at dawn I saw prayers like a luminous bubble, expanding, enlarging, everywhere; enveloping Holly. I felt immense gratitude for the love and concern expressed by so many people, for the bubbles all around us.

As always, I called TCVPO to speak to her nurse. That morning it was Barb on duty, and she reported, "Holly's very stable." So hopeful! A gentle snow was falling on Charlottesville that morning.

Later in the day, our friends José and Lourdes called from their home in Bogotá, Colombia. They were praying and offering Masses for Holly's recovery. They were devout Roman Catholics who once brought Holly a vial of Holy Water from the Church of the Holy Sepulchre in Jerusalem. She kept it on the nightstand beside her bed at home.

They were among the several South American Naval officers and their spouses that Tim became friends with during his years chasing tall ships on behalf of Norfolk's harbor. Tim had had a couple of grand adventures stemming from his friendship with José, not the least of which was a once-in-a-lifetime trip to Bogotá to judge the Miss

Columbia beauty pageant. José and Lourdes, who had a daughter of their own, as well as a son, took a special interest in our Holly. They were fond of Tim, and he returned their affection. The commandant of the Colombian Navy awarded a Distinguished Service Medal to Tim. The medal and the proclamation are in a drawer in my bedroom, safely tucked between some old tee shirts. An odd spot, I admit, yet they seem now to be from another lifetime.

Snow continued to fall throughout that day. In the afternoon, some of the transplant team came into the waiting room and sat with us. They assured us they were not giving up on Holly. They reported that she was maintaining her blood pressure as fluids were drained from her body.

Reassured, I entered her cubicle in TCVPO after receiving the nurse's permission. I held Holly's hands and massaged her arms. I rubbed her feet, which she often liked me to do when she wasn't feeling well. The bed she was in had the intricate electrical ability to undulate at specified intervals, like waves on the ocean, so that pressure on her body would not be too intense in any one spot. That bed seemed almost as sensitive as my own hands.

Our daily routine was to stay at the hospital until late in the evening and then head back to Leicester for some rest.

When I woke up Friday morning, I made my customary call to the nurse in TCVPO. Holly's primary nurse informed me, "Last night's x-ray looked significantly worse. Her lungs are white as a tee shirt."

I started to cry, but then Tim reminded me, "She's not gone!"

He was strong for us both. I'll always be grateful for the inner resources he called upon during those dreadful days. And that morning he was right. Holly was not gone.

As long as she had not been pronounced dead, there was hope. She could still recover. She could still come back to us. From the remnants of my religious education, I recalled the scripture in the Gospel of Mark when Jesus tells His disciples, "With mortals it is impossible, but not with God; for all things are possible with God." I tried to cling to this assurance, and I tried to pray for Holly and for the donor and the donor's family, too.

It was November 22. Seven days had passed since the lung transplant. We had not seen our daughter awake or conscious for one week. Sometime that day, one of the surgeons "went back into her lungs" (his phrase) and told us they looked good, inside and out. I'm not sure now what this meant. It was just that morning that her nurse told us the x-rays looked "significantly worse." But it was much easier to hear the positive than the negative. Every moment that she was still alive was a moment of hope. Every additional medical procedure, large or small, brought with it the expectation of good news.

That Friday, my friends Marcia and Barbara drove up from Suffolk, bringing a picnic basket filled with crackers and cheese, tea bags, sparkling apple cider, and a copy of Sarah Ban Breathnach's book of daily wisdom, *Simple Abundance*. I remember that I was sitting in the waiting room, crowded at midday with other families, when my two friends walked in. I was so glad to see them both. Carefully, they navigated me to a coffee shop near UVA grounds. It turned out to be crowded, too, and noisy with the exuberance of young students. What a ruthless contrast to my comatose daughter just down the street! So my friends steered me around the corner to a quieter café where a cup of hot soup for lunch nourished my numb body.

Friendship was not only essential to me as I moved through tragedy, it has proved irreplaceable ever after. Barbara, an energetic, beautiful brunette with a witty sense of humor, holds a special place in my heart. As it sometimes happens, Barbara's life and mine have drifted apart. But all these years after that dismal November day in Charlottesville, I still remember her fondly. Marcia, a quiet red-haired lady, remains a close friend to this day.

On Saturday, November 23, I woke up early and wrote:

> *Last night I dreamt that Holly opened her eyes.*

The reality was that she still lay in a coma, eyes shut in a swollen face. Her tongue stuck out of her mouth. I tried to soothe her cracked lips and tongue with Vaseline. I longed for her to open her eyes and look at me. *Please, just one more time!* My desperate prayers for my daughter's healing continued. *Please, please come back!*

Many friends and family members came to visit, to sit with us and to see Holly. As they emerged from her small space, singly or in pairs, I noticed that mostly they looked so sad.

What's the matter with them? I wondered to myself. *Don't they see she's getting better?*

But there was the time in the family waiting room—I sat on a sofa writing something in my journal—when unexpectedly and from who knows where, a scream came out of my mouth.

"Please don't take my daughter away from me!" I shrieked. "I'll go insane!"

Tim and his sister Violet rushed to comfort me, while others, friends and strangers, just stared.

Later that evening, Tim prepared to ride with his sisters back to Suffolk. He wanted to pick up some work to do at the hospital while we waited. He planned to drive back, so that meant we'd have two cars in Charlottesville. Before they left, his sister Gwen was talking on the phone to her husband. I heard her say, "It doesn't look good."

I thought, *I know she isn't talking about Holly.*

Sunday morning, the 24th, I woke up alone in the guest room at Leicester. It was a bright and sunny morning, and I knew that in churches all over the place, prayers would be offered for Holly's complete and quick recovery. I prayed that the transplanted donor lungs, so generously given, would feel comfortable in their new home.

Holly was still unconscious in her undulating bed when I saw her that morning. A huge bandage still covered her entire chest, and tape holding tubes inserted into her groin and neck was still there. Her bloated face had tubing taped into her nose. Her hands were positioned at her sides as if she were loosely holding onto the mattress. I read to her. I read every word of every card and every note of good wishes that people had sent. I described flower arrangements and balloon bouquets to her. Did she hear? I like to think so.

The rollercoaster of hope and desperation continued. One day, I was rubbing her feet and legs, her elegant dancer's feet elevated in what looked like moon-walking space boots. Purple splotches appeared on her feet and lower legs. The nurse told me those splotches meant blood vessels were bursting, and I couldn't rub her legs any more. That was a terrible moment. More and more I was helpless to do anything that might help my daughter.

Tim had planned to return that evening but called to

say he was going to stay home until the next morning. He had some things to do and phone calls to make. I was fine with that. We'd been very close during this ordeal, and I was so grateful for his sobriety and strength.

~

Here comes the confessional. I don't want to remember this, but it's good that I do. If this were a how-to book, perhaps *101 Favorite Coping Strategies for When Your Child Is Dying*, the incident that follows would fall under the category of What Absolutely Not to Do.

First, let me set the stage with an event that had occurred almost twenty years earlier. The year was 1977, and my father suffered a stroke at the age of sixty-three. My two little girls were seven and three. One morning, I got a phone call that Dad's condition was critical. I flew to California to be with my mother and my two younger sisters, Jan and Emmy, in San Clemente.

I remember walking from one concourse to another at O'Hare in Chicago to change planes. As I walked through the crowds, in my mind I pieced together my parents' early relationship. I imagined their meeting at a church in Richmond, Virginia, where Mother played the organ and Father sang tenor solo. I wondered about their four-year prim and proper courtship, their official engagement on Easter Sunday, and their elegant formal wedding in Richmond on October 13, 1939.

I prayed that my father would survive this crisis.

Arriving in the afternoon at the Orange County airport in California, I was met by Emmy's husband. He drove me to San Clemente General Hospital, a pretty little one-story facility designed with overtones of Spanish architecture.

There my father lay in a bed with rails up around his body, conscious but ill. I remember he looked so gray, and I don't mean his hair. I took his hand, and placed it over my heart. He smiled, happy to see me. For several days, he remained in critical condition, and my sisters and I stayed with our mother at the hospital most of the day and went home to Mom's in the evenings.

Mother was distraught, not ready to lose the security of her husband. Emmy was pregnant with her second child, and there was conflict between her and her husband. He felt that she was spending too much time away from him and their two-year-old son. Jan was alternately effusive in her welcoming of me and angry with me for what she perceived to be my lack of feeling.

"Terry's been crying," Emmy protested when Jan flew at me with the accusation, "Don't you even care?"

I suppose the strength during crisis that I would need later was already in evidence.

Actually, we laughed a lot. We were the Reed girls, and sarcastic laughter was always the Reed family's defensive refuge. One night our Aunt Dottie and her two daughters, Sharon and Pattie, were with us at Mom's spacious apartment. We played Pounce, a card game traditional to our family and one of our chief methods of connecting with one another. We also shared a large bottle of sherry. I most definitely overindulged. The result was that I went to bed tipsy and woke up with a severe headache the next morning. That very night, Dad turned the corner and began to get well.

After Tim called to say he would stay home until the next morning, Sandra and I decided to have a grown-up ladies' pajama party, complete with popcorn and wine, at

Leicester. And, after the wine was gone, whatever else we could find in Sandra's well-stocked liquor cabinet.

There was a certain misguided method in the madness that ensued that night at Sandra's. We let our hair down. We bonded. We drank ourselves silly. I honestly thought, in the twisted desperation of my grief over Holly, that if it worked for my father, it would work for my daughter, too. If I could drown out my own extreme anxiety with alcohol, get my mind into a state where I let go of the wretched fear, then sleep it off; somehow, that would allow Holly to heal. That was my distorted thinking.

Unfortunately, all I did was make myself sick. I woke up the next morning with a hangover the likes of which I had never experienced before and will never again. My head throbbed and my stomach churned. I was miserable.

Nevertheless, I went to the hospital that Monday morning. At one point during the day, I was in TCVPO standing next to Holly's bed, gazing at her. Two respiratory therapists whom I had not met before came in to check on the ECMO machine. The earlier attempt to wean her from the ECMO had been unsuccessful. The therapists were nice women, professional, friendly, caring. I hoped they did not detect my dreadful dissolute condition. I'll never know if they caught a whiff of the previous night's stale alcohol.

I suffered for my foolishness all day long. At eight o'clock that night, with no improvement in Holly's condition, I wrote in my journal, *I have managed to survive this hung-over day.* And I made a pact with myself never to tell Tim about the night of stupid debauchery. Tim was as sober as a judge during those days.

At six in the morning of Tuesday, November 26, I wrote a brief prayer in my journal:

Dear God,
Please open Holly's eyes today.
Open her eyes and let her walk and dance.

I remember driving to the hospital on that sunny, cold morning. I drove into the parking garage, parked the car, crossed the street, and walked into the hospital lobby where I glanced at Kacey Carneal's happy folk art paintings. Kacey was artist-in-residence at the Kluge Rehabilitation Center for Children at UVA, and her work was on display. Each frame was a unique extension of the painting. Even in my distraught state, her art intrigued me.

I'd like to meet that artist one day, I thought.

I rode the elevator up to the third floor and into the family waiting room. Aptly named. There is little that happens there but waiting. Waiting for news. Praying for good news. Sitting. Waiting.

Waiting until I could no longer wait to see my daughter again, then making the necessary phone call to request permission to enter the unit. That day I was also waiting for Tim to return, and he did, just before lunch. Our mood was morose. I tried desperately to raise my spirits by praying for faith in God's good work. I could not fathom Holly dying. I could not grasp any outcome but her healing.

Holly's primary nurse was named Samantha. She was a skilled RN who exuded compassion as well as competence. She was married to a young resident physician who was studying at the medical center. Her husband was a deer hunter who liked to use a black-powder rifle.

"The testosterone is flying," she reported of their household during those days of the November hunting season after he returned from the woods with a deer. I don't know why I remember that so vividly.

I also remember her coming into the family room that Tuesday night, after a couple of days off. We'd missed her. I was sitting on the floor. I have no idea why. Tim sat in a chair nearby. Samantha plopped herself down on the floor with me. We sat cross-legged, facing each other.

She looked directly into my eyes. "You know I haven't seen Holly in two days."

"Yes," I said.

"When I walked in today," she said, "it seemed her soul was already gone."

I stared at her. Nodded. I knew what she was saying to me. She was telling me Holly would die soon, but still I couldn't consciously acknowledge that possibility. Actually, I felt grateful to her for her honesty, but Tim told me later that her comment annoyed him. "She took away what hope we had left," he said.

Not my hope.

Sobbing and sobbing that night at Sandra's, I called Dr. E, who had been my psychiatrist since 1982, a few months after Heather died. I left a message on her answering machine, and very soon she returned my call. She was in Charlottesville, it turned out, helping with her new granddaughter.

"Dr. E, please call Holly's doctors," I begged her. "Tell them they have to make her get well. Please! Call Samantha, please!"

"You want me to call her at home?" asked Dr. E.

"No. She's at work all night."

Dr. E spoke to Samantha, and then called me back. "That young woman is all heart," she commented.

She told me that Samantha had explained what was going on from the medical standpoint. I didn't ask her for details, and I don't remember the rest of our conversation, but she soothed me. I know I felt calmer after our conversation. I went to sleep.

The next day was Wednesday, November 27, the day before Thanksgiving. I slept later than usual, and when I woke, I wrote a letter to Holly:

> Holly my Love,
>
> I'm still out at Sandra's this morning. When I first woke up, I felt sick. With your dad's help I've nursed my body back to health as I wish I could do for you. Your dad brought me some good coffee and a bowl of cereal, which I ate, up here in bed. Dad is leaving to see you now, and I'll be there after a while.
>
> I love you, Holly,
>
> Mom

I spoke with the morning nurse, Donna, who told me that Holly was keeping up her blood pressure while they gradually tried—again—to wean her from the ECMO. To me that meant that Holly was coming back. I was happy, for a little while.

We played music for Holly almost constantly on a cassette player. We kept her entertained with Celine Dion, Ten Thousand Maniacs, and Deana Carter. Once, with Tim on one side of the bed and me on the other, "Strawberry Wine" was playing.

He said to her, "Listen, they're playing our song."

Our song—ours—the three of us. We had sung that song on a road trip a couple of years before, and we'd laughed at ourselves as we sang.

People began drifting in. Tim's nephew Bob and his wife,

Lynda, were there, and his niece Diana came. Holly's boyfriend, Scott, out of college for the Thanksgiving weekend, drove up with his sister and mother. Her cousins Brenda and Andrea were with us.

The pulmonologist walked in.

"We're going back into her lungs," he said. "We'll try to jump-start them again."

Jump-starting would work! I was so sure. While they jump-started Holly's lungs, I walked out into the hall. The door to TCVPO where they worked was wide open. Bright, bright lights flooded her bed, and a bevy of hospital personnel swirled around her.

I returned to the waiting room, my hopes high. After a while, the doctor came out and said it wasn't working.

Brightly, I answered, "We'll just try again tomorrow."

He shook his head.

Then two surgeons, along with the pulmonologist and a nurse, took Tim and me into the same conference room where, twelve days before, they had told us she was getting worse after her transplant. It was a small, square room, with several chairs and a lamp on an end table.

"There's nothing more we can do," one of the surgeons said.

He told us that the bursting blood vessel activity manifesting on her legs was probably going on in her brain as well.

"Her brain?" I moaned. I screamed. "Nobody loses two children in one lifetime. Nobody! It's inhuman!"

No one else said anything, yet I was keenly aware that Tim, beside me, was linked tightly to me, silent though he seemed. For a moment our two hearts melded and became one in our mutual incomprehensible heartbreak.

Desolate, we trudged back to the waiting room, prepared to stay there all night. We didn't know when the end would come, but we knew it would be within a few hours. It came sooner.

Tim and I stood at Holly's bedside when Samantha turned off her life support equipment. The monitors went flat. In one stinging moment she was dead.

We went out into the waiting room and sat, stunned.

Soon Samantha came to get us. She had removed the tape and tubes from Holly's body. She had cleaned our daughter and straightened the bed. We said goodbye with quiet music playing in the background. Scott came in and stroked her face. Others were in and out, weeping.

Holly's ordeal ended. Our vigil ended, but not our suffering.

We all went out to Sandra's, where Tim's niece made coffee. It was after midnight, so I don't know why. Someone had brought a pie. Maybe they needed a midnight snack. But Tim and I went to bed, and I think we slept. The morning of Thanksgiving Day our pastor knelt beside my bed.

Opening my eyes, I looked at him and said, "This wasn't supposed to happen, was it?'

"No."

In my journal, I wrote:

> *Last night Holly died about 11:30. She was ready to be with her sister. I would love to have kept her with us. But her soul made a different choice. Be at Peace, Holly. You are Home now.*

And I prayed that Tim and I would be given the loving comfort that our broken hearts needed.

CHAPTER EIGHT

The Second Funeral

I thought thy bride-bed to have deck'd, sweet maid,
And not have strew'd thy grave.

—*Hamlet,* act 5, scene 1

"The service is going to be at St. Paul's Church on Saturday," Tim reported to me after discussing the arrangements with our pastor and the funeral home director.

That was a good idea. St. Paul's was not our parish, but it's a larger church and it's right on Main Street in downtown Suffolk. Our own little St. John's, on the other hand, is tiny and tucked away on a rural road in the Chuckatuck section of the city.

My memory of Thanksgiving morning is vague. After the priest came to my bedside to comfort me, I must have gotten dressed and said farewell to Sandra and her family. I remember the previous night, being in the family waiting room after Holly died. So many of the staff from around the hospital came to hug us and offer their condolences. Some were crying. I was not. I was too numb to cry. Heartbroken, yet emotionally anesthetized. Tim was heartbroken too, but in his take-charge mode. Thank God! I couldn't have taken charge of boiling an egg.

"Do you want to have her cremated?" he asked.

I thought for a moment. "No."

Tim drove my car home from Charlottesville. Just as after Heather's death, I could not drive. A nephew drove Tim's car. On the way home, exhaustion overwhelmed me, yet I couldn't doze off. My head ached. I felt uncomfortable in my skin. I couldn't relax and rest.

"Let's write her obituary," suggested Tim.

Together we wrote a fitting and meaningful tribute. Mostly, Tim dictated and I wrote it down. Tim was a wordsmith when he let Spirit instead of spirits move him. The latter had yet to take over his life. Spirit helped pull us through those days of sorrow.

Somehow we ended up at my sister-in-law Violet's for Thanksgiving dinner. My sister Emmy and her daughter Jade had flown in from California. Someone, I don't know who, met them at the airport. The three of us were sitting at the kitchen table when Gwen, another of Tim's sisters, wandered over, kissed me, and said, "I love you."

Later, at home, I lay in bed weeping. I called to Emmy, "Please get Tim for me."

Tim came and sat on the bed. Through my sobs I begged, "Please bring her back!"

"I wish I could." His sorrow was palpable.

In the obituary, we had stated that two pastors would be officiating, one of whom we'd been unable to contact due to the holiday. The reverend we were missing was a chaplain at Children's Hospital of the Kings Daughters. An ordained Baptist minister, she was progressive and forward thinking. She had been close to Holly, and to me as well. We did finally contact her.

"I'd be honored to participate in Holly's service," she said.

On that longest Friday after Thanksgiving Thursday, she and the priest from St. John's came to the house to plan the funeral. I wore an old green robe over my nightgown, and we sat in the living room. Tim had left to deliver the eulogy to the local newspapers.

My mind flashed back to an earlier time when Heather was newly dead, and I had remarked to another pastor, "Isn't it her wedding I should be helping to plan, not her funeral?"

I had a copy of the ceremony we'd held at Emmanuel Church in Virginia Beach in January 1982 for Heather. We decided to repeat that liturgy—the same hymns, same biblical passages, same non-scripture readings to include the passage "On Children" from *The Prophet* and Henry Van Dyke's poem "Gone from My Sight." This time though, instead of the priest reading these last two, I said that Tim and I would like to do it ourselves. The two ministers looked at me, startled.

"Are you sure?"

"Absolutely sure. Tim's going to read the poem, and I'm going to read from *The Prophet.* I'm also going to read Kahlil Gibran's passage 'On Death.'"

The question of whether to have Communion came up. Heather's service had not included Eucharist.

"Do you practice an open Communion?" the hospital chaplain asked our priest.

He nodded. All would be welcome, regardless of creed or denomination, to take part in the sacrament.

"Let's do Communion," she said.

Meanwhile, people were in and out of our house bringing food and flowers. We'd developed a diverse group of friends, neighbors, and co-workers, covering a lot of ground on the philosophical and religious spectrum. On their way out the front door, one conservative couple offered their opinion that Holly's death was God's will. Immediately, another friend walked in through the kitchen bearing a casserole and commenting, "This is easier to understand if you believe in reincarnation."

In my wobbly emotional state, I wanted to laugh at the seeming absurdity of it all. Reincarnation? God's will? We're getting ready to bury another daughter! Who could ever make meaning of such a loss, such losses?

I will say, though, that every single expression of condolence, in whatever form, was appreciated. If there's ever doubt about what to do when a friend or acquaintance has lost a loved one, I can say that almost anything will help. I cherished every card, each phone call. The lasagnas, fruit salads, ham sandwiches, and chocolate cakes—we were grateful for all of them. The food was welcome, and I loved these good people, all wanting to help. Yet I knew that nothing could make any difference in the long run. It was bewildering to me. I was not angry then. I had been angry and would be again, but in the immediate aftermath of both the girls' deaths, I was perplexed at finding myself in such circumstances. I could only nod nicely when people spoke to me or came to visit. I felt like an alien from a faraway land.

The night before the funeral, we'd been at Baker Funeral

Home greeting people. Holly's coffin sat open while people walked by. I didn't like the open casket custom any more than I had the first time, but as when Heather died, I realized it would be important to some folks. I noticed, as lines of mourners streamed by, that some didn't look in her casket.

They don't believe her soul is there either. What's in the casket is an empty shell, I thought.

I became so exhausted during that Friday night that finally my legs and feet wouldn't hold me up, even though I wore clunky L.L. Bean clogs. As the last of the visitors filed by, I plopped down in a chair and wondered how I'd get up again. Someone must have helped me. I ended up back home somehow.

Saturday morning was cold and windy. The funeral was to start at eleven. The funeral director came to get us in a limousine. He sat in the living room with Tim. Out of the corner of my eye and my mind, I was aware that some financial matters were being discussed. Did Tim write a check right then and there? That would seem cold. Does my memory play tricks on me?

Once again I said to myself, *Thank You, God, for Tim's strength now.*

I was getting dressed in a black suit and a black hat. I couldn't figure out what shoes to wear. They had to be flat or I would topple over. I settled on some gold flats I'd bought on sale in a Charlottesville shoe store some months prior. Just so they didn't look too outlandish, I carried a small black bag with a gold shoulder strap. I pulled the veil of the hat down over my eyes.

Then Tim, Emmy, her soon-to-be-ex-husband, her daughter Jade, and I were driven to St. Paul's Episcopal

Church in the big black funeral limo. When we arrived in the parking lot and got out of the car, I saw the hearse. I blurted out to whomever was around, "This doesn't make sense! It just doesn't make sense!" I was half numb, half afraid, and determined to get through the service.

We were ushered into a room in back of the church where the pastors, now vested, sat down at a table with us.

"If you can't do the readings, we'll do them."

I nodded. My eyes were almost closed, to shut out the reality of what was happening.

Soon Tim and I, holding hands, were walking outside and around the perimeter of the building toward the front door of the sanctuary. The church bells rang. It was eleven o'clock. I felt very close to Tim and glad to have his hand to hold. Still, half of me was scared and the other half almost unconscious. It is so good at such a time to have people around—the church was full, and the funeral directors were doing their job, guiding us from one point to another. But during that brief walk from the parish hall to the church's front door, Tim and I were alone in the chill air, with the chiming of the bells and the aroma of boxwood in the air. We were intimately swathed in our sorrow, in a bittersweet, private moment.

Our extended families, consisting of dozens from Tim's side and three from mine, assembled in the narthex. There was a woman there who attended St. John's. She spoke with a German accent, had a French first name and an Irish last name. Renée Brady had lost one of her four sons, tragically, a few years earlier. I'd felt the kindred bond with her of one bereaved mother to another and wondered about the multinational nature of her names and accent. When she mailed a get-well card to Holly during one of her hospitalizations, the mystery unraveled. Her name was actually the Germanic Renate, Anglicized (or Francized?) when she moved to the States to join her Irish-American husband. Renée entered the narthex as we gathered for the processional.

She began to cry, saying mournfully, "I have prayed and prayed for your daughter."

I nodded my thanks. I don't think there was anyone else in the narthex who spoke to me before the service.

The organist began to play. Majestically, the pipe organ resonated with Martin Luther's early sixteenth-century hymn, "A Mighty Fortress Is Our God." "Our helper he amid the flood of mortal ills prevailing," sang the congregation as our procession moved down the aisle.

Our priest recited these words from the Book of Common Prayer: "I am Resurrection and I am Life, says the Lord," while we all remained standing in acknowledgement of Holly's casket, borne into the church by the pall bearers.

What is it that I remember about Holly's funeral? Do I remember walking down the aisle with Tim? Not really. I remember sitting in that front pew on the left side of the aisle. I remember the church being full. I remember that I felt my eyes were very dark, as if my pupils were enlarged so there was only black and no green iris to be seen. How in the world would I know anything like that? Yet that's the image I have of myself, that I was swallowed by grief, outside myself and at the same time deep into myself and my indescribable sorrow, aware of things going on around me yet not aware, all at the same time. Was I outside myself looking in? I was mourning, yet I was not crying. I was engulfed in grief next to Tim, who was also engulfed in grief.

Who sat on the left side of me? My sister? I think so. I think Tim and I held hands as we walked in, following a long line of mourners. We sat down. We celebrated Holly's life.

I got up to read from *The Prophet* and there was silence throughout the church. Silence! I think no one could believe I could do it. I had to do it and am glad I did. It was my tribute to my beautiful daughter whom I loved so much.

Then I watched the people going up for Communion. It took a long time, all those people who had come to say goodbye. Goodbye, Holly. Friends and relatives and medical people from CHKD and our friends in Charlottesville and people I barely remembered from years ago in Norfolk.

Her schoolmates. Kelly brought her new baby. Holly's boyfriend, Scott, with his mom and sister, was there. Her would-be boyfriend, Paul, from ninth grade, who had looked crestfallen one day when he came over to see her but she wasn't home. Stacie and Trennie and people I worked with. Rose and Flora, other teachers. Alva, who later buried her husband, and Barbara—friends still, but we don't get together much any more. Other parents of children with CF. Men clapped Tim on the shoulder on their way from the altar. A woman kissed the coffin.

It was a long, long service.

Later we stood in the narthex with the doors open to the cold blustery November air as people filed by. We didn't plan that reception line. It just happened. But it was good to greet those who had attended, to hug them and be hugged.

It had been an interminable three days since Holly had died.

At the funeral, in addition to the teaching "On Children," I read from the teaching "On Death." *The Prophet* said of Death, "For life and death are one, even as the river and the sea are one. In the depth of your hopes and desires lies your silent knowledge of the beyond."

There was and remains so much in this passage from Kahlil Gibran that is meaningful: "And what is it to cease breathing, but to free the breath from its restless tides, that it may rise and expand and seek God unencumbered?"

How fitting for my young daughter who died because she couldn't breathe properly.

Holly's entire little chest was encased in thick bandaging during her final comatose days. I'd been afraid to touch the dressing, which was probably ten or twelve inches wide and wrapped around her body, for fear of damaging some of the surgeon's intricate work.

As I read the words from *The Prophet,* I thought of that, and how she was freed of confining bandages and of the restless tides of insufficient breath. Then the final sentence: "When the earth shall claim your limbs, then shall you truly dance."

I envisioned her in a space I'd once seen in a dream. In that dream, Heather came to me after her death. Golden curtains parted, and she came down a ladder from a place of bright light. She was dressed in a robe of such exquisite blue that, look as I may, I have never found that hue duplicated here on earth. Her head was wrapped in a turban. She was serene and beautiful and full of life. We longed to communicate, but we were permitted only a scant acknowledgment of each other before she was led back up the ladder into a place where I knew there was glorious peacefulness beyond my comprehension. That brief glimpse that

I was given of Heaven's anteroom remained indescribably precious and vivid years later. The words from *The Prophet* took me there and I saw Holly dancing, her legs strong, perfect, and free from blood splotches.

Holly had gone to that place she wrote about on her last day of consciousness, a place where God and her grandmother and Heather welcomed her.

CHAPTER NINE

Guns and Clutter

Canst thou not minister to a mind diseas'd,
Pluck from the memory a rooted sorrow,
Raze out the written troubles of the brain
And with some sweet oblivious antidote
Cleanse the stuff'd bosom of that perilous stuff
Which weighs upon the heart?

—*Macbeth*, act 5, scene 3

Holly's body in its casket was sent to a mortuary in Morehead City. The casket was opened again for North Carolina family and friends who couldn't come to Suffolk for the first viewing and grieving. I remained in a detached fog at the funeral home.

Someone said, "She's cute."

Cute? What a nonsensical thing to say about the corpse of my daughter!

Exhaustion set in again. I looked at the clock and thought, *I can make it through one more hour.*

And then to God, "Give me the strength to live through the next thirty minutes."

Holly was buried in the North Carolina Cemetery in Broad Creek, where her grandparents and her sister had been laid to rest.

On our last of three days in Broad Creek, one of my four sisters-in-law said, "Tim seems so calm. I bet he'll fall apart when this is over."

Gee, thanks for those reassuring words, I thought. I wanted to smack her.

I prayed for help to keep going for ten more minutes, when we would get in our car and leave.

We drove home in near silence to our sad home.

And then we were two.

~

This was not what the empty nest was supposed to feel like. Not such a huge cavernous void. Not such deep gashes in our hearts. As time moved on, we covered our raw wounds with the emotional bandage of busyness, hoping to staunch the bleeding. But our hearts continued to bleed.

In the interconnected web that crosses space and time, Shakespeare's words at the beginning of this chapter spoke to me. Here we find Macbeth, feudal lord and later king in eleventh-century Scotland, imploring a doctor to cure his ailing wife. Lady Macbeth has become deluded, delirious, and plagued by demonic visions. The six lines quoted above became a mantra of desperation for me, as I watched my husband's mental state spiral downward.

We had good times as well as bad, Tim and I, and the months and years stretched out. We traveled a bit—to Pennsylvania Amish country and Gettysburg one summer, and to the coast of Oregon to spend Christmas with my mother. We drove across the country in our Vanagon. In Santa Fe, we witnessed the most glorious sunset ever; the entire sky was an eye-popping panorama of pink, gold, and purple, like colors from a richer world. We made love with immense tenderness in the Mohave Desert. Tears streamed down both our faces afterward, and we held each other close for a long time.

One day, Tim was going through files in his home office. He came across Holly's death certificate and handed it to me. "Do you want to keep this thing?" he asked.

I grabbed it and ran up the stairs screaming, "No! No! No! It's not true. She's not dead. It's not true."

I threw myself down on the floor of the landing and sobbed.

After a few minutes, I calmed down and put the death certificate back in the file.

For me, life would go on. I'd walk through my heart's death valley and keep going. I'd be reborn. The deeply rooted sorrow took strong hold in Tim's soul. There was yet another dying for me to live through.

The doctor answered Macbeth: "Therein the patient must minister to himself."

I pondered these words and their meaning as Tim became more and more despondent. I know that working through grief is hard. A little escape, a little denial, can be helpful. Briefly we escape the *reality* of grief in our lives and in so doing we reach the authentic *truth* of our lives. The reality was that the anguish I felt as a bereaved mother was one hair's breadth away from being unbearable. The truth was that the hair's breadth of space contained life. The reality was that life without my daughters sometimes felt like traveling through a threatening maze formed from the sharp edges of sadness. The truth was that I was given the strength to find a healthy way through the maze.

Consider some of the ways we try to escape the web of grief. There is destructive behavior, like overindulgence in drugs and alcohol. Then there are positive behaviors, like meditation and daydreaming, reveries of the imagination, immersion in a novel or a movie. Briefly escaping from reality, we come back refreshed, renewed, and rejuvenated. A little sojourn softens the sharp edges without taking away the truth.

Tim, unfortunately, never found any healthy strategies that he could stick with to deal with grief. In the manner of independent males of his generation, especially (I think) those raised in the rural south, he was reluctant to seek help. There is a passage in *Darkness Visible,* William Styron's short memoir dealing with depression and alcoholism, where he addresses his aversion to therapeutic techniques. I saw that same aversion in Tim.

On occasion, in deep despondency, Tim did seek help. Usually he tried through power of will to remain sane and healthy—what the twelve-step programs call "white knuckling." Always, he slipped back into what I named the Three Ds. This became my private code identifying a cycle of behavior. First, the Depression increased. Next the heavy Drinking resumed. The Drinking merely served to intensify the Depression, and soon he was floundering in his Drunk Depressed Doldrums. The Three Ds.

Twice his friends and colleagues from downtown Norfolk came and dragged him to the hospital. The first time, his sisters and I helped. The second time it happened without me, while I was at work. Both times we all thought that a brief stay in a psychiatric hospital would help him. I had high hopes each time that the transformative effects would be permanent. "Therein the patient must minister to himself." We tossed the ball into his court. He couldn't hit it back.

Tim was at his best when he had a project to work on. Projects energized him and gave him purpose. Between projects, he seemed to lose his grounding.

Tim seemed to me to be a person larger than life. Larger-than-life people are not always easy to live with. Over the top, imposing, impressive, charismatic, creative, interesting, and infuriating are some adjectives that come to mind as I try to describe the essence of Tim, but never "easy."

~

Thirty-five years had passed since my first kitchen conversation with Tim's mother, the time she told me about losing her baby. The pathos repeated one day when Tim stood in the kitchen of our Suffolk home, his joie de vivre obliterated by the tragedies our marriage had sustained.

"I'm hollow," he said to me. "I'm empty from my neck to my knees."

I said nothing.

"I'm getting ready to blow my brains out." The flat statement was made without emotion.

"When are you going to do that?" I asked.

"In a few minutes."

"Oh. Well."

What else could I say or do that had not already been said and done? *This, too, shall pass,* I thought to myself.

The next morning, Tim lay on his stomach in our cherrywood bed. I was sleeping in another room by then. He wore a dingy tee shirt that clung to his body like a sweaty old rag. His head, with silver hair askew, twisted round on his neck like a turtle in response to my whispering his name. He looked at me with eyes crazed and inward focused, but with remnants of tenderness in his small psychotic smile.

"Please, Honey," I begged. "Please let me take you to the hospital."

He muttered, "No. No more hospitals. No more doctors."

It was Thursday of my spring break from school. I went upstairs to my loft study and tried to read. Truthfully, I was in despair; for I saw his suffering and was helpless to help him. Silently, I begin to recite the Twenty-third Psalm. Its reassurance of love and safety had bolstered me in previous dark times.

Then. Crackbang! A pistol shot pounded through the silence of the house. An icy shock ran up my spine and into my scalp. The odor of gunpowder permeated the air.

I ran to the balcony overlooking the living room and what I saw was my husband's chest with blood running down the front of his tee shirt. I screamed. I rushed downstairs and phoned my next-door neighbors. I sat on the back porch and waited for them. We entered the kitchen where the couple propped me into a chair at the table. The husband went into the living room.

"My God, he's shot half his head off," I heard him say.

Can his head be put back together? Like Humpty Dumpty. The absurd thought popped into my head.

Then my neighbor returned to the kitchen and asked me, "Have you called the police?"

I stared at him through a nightmarish dream haze. The neighbor called the police.

"No," I heard him say, obviously in response to a police question. "I am certain the wife did not do it."

~

Later I decided that a miracle had happened. Some supernatural force had prevented me from seeing anything above Tim's neck when I looked over the railing, because, truly, there seemed a curtain covering his head.

In point of fact, a bullet had smashed my husband's brain case, shattering its contents in an explosion of bloody debris that littered our living room and sprayed our walls. In a heartbeat of time on Maundy Thursday, life was forever altered. There was an instant of clarity in which my soul understood my husband's freedom from unbearable pain, and then I began a long downward trip into the underworld.

My psychiatrist explained, "For a second, you saw his head, and then you dissociated and amnesia set in. It was too horrible for your psyche to deal with."

Supernatural or not, dissociative amnesia or not, it still seems a miracle. Years later, I have no memory of having seen his smashed skull, and that's a memory I never need to retrieve. The horror of it would be too great. Telling this story, years after his suicide, the agitation and consternation I feel startles me. I thought I had worked through the trauma, made my peace, come to terms with it. Yet the horror of the moment returns, fresh and raw.

T. S. Eliot ended his famous poem "The Hollow Men" with the following frequently quoted lines:

This is the way the world ends
Not with a bang but a whimper.

Tim's was a histrionic ending to a theatrical life. He left us not with a whimper but with a bang.

And then there was me.

CHAPTER TEN

The Third Funeral

To die, to sleep,
No more; and by a sleep . . . we end
The heartache.

—*Hamlet,* act 3, scene 1

Tim and I were arguing one day, several years after Holly's death. Over what, I have no idea. It's immaterial now. We were two sad people, two brokenhearted parents, an angry husband and an angry wife.

I said, "You know what we do really well together? We do good funerals."

"Oh, come on, Babe," he said. "That's ridiculous."

"Oh no," said I. "A good funeral is one thing we can count on doing right every time."

~

I had nothing to do with Tim's memorial service. I was in shock. His friends and colleagues from downtown Norfolk arranged the event, held in Town Point Park on the Norfolk waterfront that Tim loved, on April 23, 2001. Shakespeare's birthday is traditionally observed on April 23, and the bard died on April 23, 1616. This piece of trivia didn't enter into the planning of the ceremony, but it struck me as significant. I have a way of seeing signs and wonders everywhere—connection, serendipity, and synchronicity.

The memorial service was almost lavish. Locally known singers performed "Amazing Grace," "On Eagle's Wings," and "Over the Rainbow." Company members from the Williamsburg repertory theater, who now lived far away, reunited to present a portion of *Spoon River Anthology*. It was a piece that that Tim had performed when he was with that theater. Speakers from our local area and from other states remembered my husband—a college classmate, a former student, a retired Coast Guard captain from Massachusetts, a retired bank president from Virginia, and the executive director of FestEvents, the organization that oversees Town Point Park events. Tim's nephew remembered his uncle wearing a beret in the 1960s. "I didn't know people in Virginia were allowed to wear berets and beards in those days," he joked. The large audience chuckled. The celebration of Tim's life was abundantly attended.

Not only was the service on Shakespeare's birthday, but each of our three deaths occurred on a day of some annual significance. *How thoughtful of my dear family members,* I said to myself in a sarcastic moment. First, there was January 18, 1982, which was Martin Luther King Day that particular year. Second, there was Thanksgiving Eve, just before midnight on November 27, 1996. (My husband's desk calendar remained on that date until his death. Did his life actually stop when our second daughter died?) Finally, there was April 12, 2001, Maundy Thursday. So forever afterward, as long as I live, I will grieve and mourn and remember deaths and funerals in conjunction with these commemorative days.

Interlude

I go, and it is done; the bell invites me.

—*Macbeth*, act 2, scene 1

After each death, I went deep into an area of pre-intellectual knowing, of heart knowing. On the surface, I seemed on a level plane. Tediously and with minimum show of sorrow, I went through the motions of living. But deep in my psyche, a flurry of activity raged. There, memories were color essences in jewel tones embedded in the chakras, emerging from the pulsating dark red root firmly connected to Gaia the Earth Mother and surging through all energy centers to the transpersonal chakra, above the crown of the head. It seemed I was in an underworld place.

The underworld came to me in dreams, and the dream world came to me in waking states, especially during times of solitude or meditation.

What was it like in this strange place I inhabited privately, deep in my being? In dreams, there was darkness above and below, yet there were cavelike rooms, well-lit and comfortable. In the dream rooms, there sometimes appeared gargoyles and demons. I couldn't escape. It wasn't hell, though.

Hell was the mind-numbing, shocking suicide of my husband that catapulted me into the strange dark place. Hell was watching Holly lying in a coma as her spirit and her breath left her body. Hell was witnessing the cruel deterioration of Heather's body as she gasped for breath until the final moment of her painful death.

The dying, dying, and dying of loved ones catapulted me into a netherworld where I languished. It was a lonely place, and I know now that I needed to experience the loneliness and solitude for my soul's healing to be accomplished.

I also understand now that all three of my loved ones knew they were dying, and all three of them told me. When Heather said, "Mommy, I'm going to die this year," I heard, but I didn't listen. When Holly jotted her note on the way toward her transplant surgery, when she told us she'd be fine with her sister, her grandmother, and God, I heard. But I didn't listen. And when Tim said, "I'm getting ready to blow my brains out," I heard yet didn't believe it.

The three stones of their deaths dragged me down like a weight to the River Styx, into Hell, into miserable loneliness. I survived as best I could. A colleague at work quoted another one who'd asked, "Is Terry made of stone?"

A hurtful comment, I felt. Another co-worker asked, "How do you put one foot in front of the other?" Much kinder, that question was.

Was I cold and heartless that I could live in two worlds—the world of my inner being and the world outside? Sometimes I wondered. Was I a freak, a monster-mother with a rock-hard heart that enabled me to wake up every morning, put on my makeup, and go to work? To come home, feed the dogs, and work the crossword puzzles? All the while that I carried out normal activities, the scenes in my dream life played out in weird underworld settings. I didn't understand it. But I survived.

I began to study the story of Persephone and her mother, Demeter, said to be one of the most important in Hellenic mythology. The story, which spoke to my heart, follows here in an abbreviated form:

One day Persephone, a beautiful young woman, was out picking flowers. Hades, the god of the dead, abducted her and tossed her into his chariot. He hurled the chariot down into his underworld kingdom before the other gods and goddesses could stop him. Stricken with grief for her lost daughter, Demeter, who was the vibrant goddess of agriculture, refused to let the crops grow. The harvest withered. Demeter disguised herself as an old crone and roamed the earth searching for Persephone. The Olympian gods eventually intervened, allowing Persephone to rise from the netherworld and rejoin her mother for six months out of every year.

I traveled to Greece with some friends and visited Eleusis, the spot where the disguised Demeter is said to have ended up and where the Greeks held an annual festival in pre-Christian times. In explanations of the central myth of Demeter, as it was apparently played out in the Eleusinian Mysteries, Persephone is Demeter's daughter as well as Demeter's own younger self.

In philosophical moments I had asked of myself: Who is the mother, who the daughter? According to mythology, I could be both. That was oddly comforting. Being both mother and daughter, teacher and student, reinforced my belief in Oneness, Connectedness, non-Fragmentation. All abstract terms that popped into my head and helped me when I yearned to understand the incomprehensible. I knew that my tiny and helpless infants came to teach their birth mother the secrets of loving fully and unconditionally.

In mythological explanations of the netherworld, we don't stay there forever. That was a comfort—to know I would emerge into fresh air and new life.

And so it was. They were gone. They were all gone, having taught their tender, tough lessons. Was I an unwilling student, a slow learner? Did I grasp the message embedded in my loves' lifetimes? I hope so, but it was hard learning.

Later, still alone, I began to feel that I was being reincarnated in the same body within this lifetime. Although I was certainly aware of the process of reincarnation, I had never heard of this phenomenon, of reincarnation into one's present body. As the saying goes, "When the student is willing, the teacher appears." The words of a teacher came to my attention, to elucidate my gleanings and lend credibility to my expanding awareness—a woman no longer living on the earth who had been a respected spiritual teacher during her time here. Eva Broch Pierrakos was her name. She spoke in her teachings and lectures of exactly this concept, in Pathwork Guide Lecture No. 230 (1996 edition). She stated in her lecture, "But there is one phenomenon that I would like to discuss here and that is usually neglected or denied in spiritual teachings: A person who is truly on a path of accelerated development can, and frequently does, literally reincarnate in the same lifetime."

I'd been convinced of this occurrence in my own life,

but I'd been reluctant to mention it because of bizarre associations. "Ordinary" reincarnation is sufficiently out of the mainstream that I hesitated to take the concept a single mystical, metaphysical, or esoteric step further. So I was excited to read of Eva Pierrakos and her work. Other writers and researchers in past-life regression have pointed out that a near-death experience (NDE) can be a catalyst for similar transformation within one lifetime. In my own experience, the catalyst was not my own NDE but the vicarious experience of death as I traveled with my children and husband on their journeys.

My purpose in writing about intra-life reincarnation, my belief in the Oneness of life and that death is not to be feared, is twofold. First, I'm setting the stage for a later chapter, when I'll write much more about my new life. Second, I need to emphasize the paradox of recognizing my daughters' deaths as the acceptable outworking of their lives' plans, juxtaposed against my huge need for the consolation that could only come—and then just partially—from moving and memorable memorial services.

Writing about funerals thrust me into remembrance of encounters with core truths and experiences of things unseen that occur during the darkest nights of the soul. This is where we enter the place of heart knowing that existed before and beyond the intellect. Soon after I turned forty, and continuing over the next twenty years, I lived through the deaths and funerals of my daughters, my husband, and my parents. Five deaths and five ritualized memorials. My father was eulogized in a small Episcopal chapel in Oregon. My mother's very simple and private ceremony took place in the front yard of a home where we had lived during my childhood. There were the splendid

Episcopal liturgies for my daughters. Finally, there was the elaborately staged community memorial service for my husband held in Town Point Park in Norfolk, normally a venue for festivals and fun. Funerary rites are absolutely necessary for the bereaved, and I think also for the deceased as they transition into the afterlife, their gossamer spirits hovering around their services of final tribute.

There was an exhibit of funerary urns at the Chrysler Museum of Art in Norfolk, Virginia, during the summer of 2002. The exhibit, Cinerary Urns, featured the works of glass artist William Morris. Exquisitely textured, vibrantly colored, these urns of amazing beauty and spirituality stood empty upon display stands, as the artist's tribute to personal and collective grief following September 11, 2001. In an introductory piece to the exhibit, Morris wrote: "It is beyond our ideas and thoughts about death that the true mystery and beauty begin." I agree.

Part Two

CHAPTER ELEVEN

Now, by Grace

Heaven hath a hand in these events.

—*Richard II,* act 5, scene 2

Now. Now I am happy. Now I have a good life, and this seems to me to be a miraculous part of the story.

The cremated remains of my husband's half-headless body were buried in the North Carolina ground between the embalmed corpses of our two daughters. I spent evenings alone and sad.

August 2002, sixteen months after Tim killed himself, I was settled in to my marginal life of work and crossword puzzles. I'd received invitations to two social gatherings taking place a day apart. First came an invitation came to attend a friend's birthday party on a Saturday night, a surprise party celebrating one of those decade-turning milestones. The invitation requested purple outfits and red hats.

The second gathering was to take place the following day, Sunday evening. It was billed as the "First Annual

Crab Feast," sponsored by our small St. John's Church. An adults-only social gathering, a good time would be had by all. When I received the Crab Feast invitation, I'd thought, *That sounds like fun. Why not go?* So I mailed my RSVP and a check for ten dollars and put it on my calendar.

My first inclination was to pass on the birthday celebration, but when friends called and offered to drive me to the party, I said yes to that one, too. I put it on my calendar.

My calendar was far from full, but it was as full as I wanted it to be. Mostly, I went to work. It was the last week in August. The 2002–2003 school year had begun, not for students yet, but for the staff and teachers, and it was a busy time for us. My job was to mentor, train, and supervise the teachers of the emotionally disturbed children and youth with whom we worked. The position required a lot of energy; physical and mental. This was a good thing.

Weekends, I devoted my time to stocking up on groceries and reading the Sunday paper. Working the *Los Angeles Times* and the *New York Times* crosswords in Sunday's newspapers had become my solitary weekend ritual, the apex of fun in my life.

I'd learned to do crossword puzzles during the long hours of my younger daughter's lung transplant. I stayed awake all night, systematically going through a crossword puzzle book, the kind they sell in hospital gift shops. I progressed through the puzzles from easy to hard, and I learned that when my mind couldn't contain another thing, I could do crossword puzzles to avoid going crazy.

Years later, in her memoir *The Year of Magical Thinking,* Joan Didion related that she thought crossword puzzles served the same function for her during the days following her husband's unexpected death.

After Holly's death, twelve nights following the one when I learned to work crosswords, solving these puzzles had become something of an obsession.

And after Tim's suicide, working crossword puzzles went beyond ritual and became, quite literally, the highlight of my reclusive weekend life.

That August weekend in 2002, I broke my seclusion. Wearing an old purple dress and a new red hat, I rode with friends to a well-appointed home in an upscale Virginia Beach neighborhood. The beverages and food were abundant and the guests fashionably clad in the requisite color scheme. The guest of honor arrived in a chauffeur-driven limousine from which she embarked, smiling and elegant, to the pop and flash of many cameras. Music, dancing, and frivolity cranked up as the evening wore on, and I felt like a square peg in a round hole.

The next morning I wrote in my journal:

> *I don't feel upbeat, happy, or in any way euphoric this morning. I'm no longer attractive, youthful, or rhythmic in my bearing or my attitude.*
>
> *I am an old, ugly, unaccomplished woman with no family, no one to ease me into my old age or to celebrate the milestones of my life. I have no accomplishments and have done nothing remarkable with my life. I'm depressed this morning. There is nothing further to say.*

Now I see that even at this most melancholy of moments, I realized that a new beginning might be possible, because I continued:

> *Except that I know I must pick myself up and go forward somehow into a new future. I feel I may*

> *be reincarnating into the same body, in the same lifetime.*
>
> *But my grief is so deeply embedded in cell memory that I will never discharge it. Loneliness is here to stay, too. My body is crumbling under the weight of too many years of too many tragedies.*
>
> *Perhaps at my core I am and always will be a grieving widow and a bereaved mother. Perhaps having those descriptors at my core precludes me from ever again having fun at a party. From dancing and from conviviality, from merrymaking, even with a group of delightful and like-minded people as were at the jolly festive birthday party last night.*

That sad morning I felt I would grow old all alone, probably in a wheelchair. I'd been suffering with severe backaches, and had recently been diagnosed with spinal stenosis and scoliosis. Physical therapy helped a little and pain medication took the edge off temporarily, but I was uncomfortable most of the time.

The crab feast at the church was scheduled to begin at five that evening. At four o'clock, I lounged on the sofa in my pajamas, still concentrating on finishing the crossword puzzles. *From the Parlor,* a radio broadcast of sentimental songs of the Victorian era, wafted over the airwaves from our local PBS station. An empty teacup and the forlorn remnants of my lonely lunch littered the table beside me. My hair could best be described as "bedhead gone awry." Oh, dear me, I did not want to get dressed and go to the church, where I had been mostly absent for over a year.

Then a little voice popped into my head, and said, "You need to get off your butt and out of this house," and for whatever reason, I listened to that little voice. I got up off the sofa and pulled on jeans and a purple tee shirt. I chose purple because the night before I'd painted my toenails that color to go with the red hat/purple dress scenario. Sloppily, I applied a little make-up, and for the finishing touch, plopped a straw hat over my messy hair.

Driving the seven miles to our tiny Colonial church building, one of the oldest still-active houses of worship in the country, I asked myself what in the world I was doing. Why was I submitting myself to a self-conscious reemergence into social activities? "Self-conscious," because I was certain that people would look at me with pity and whisper cautionary reminders to one another about my sad life. "Reemergence," because I'd been hiding at home for sixteen months.

I pulled my car onto the church grounds. I panicked. The parking lot was full! Steeling myself, I walked into the Parish Hall. I noticed tables crowded with folks eating crabs and drinking beer like good old Episcopalians do. ("Moderation in all things" is the unofficial motto of the previously frozen chosen.) There were so many people mingling on that warm Sunday evening. So much friendliness, so much laughter and chitchat; what did I know about laughter and chatting anymore?

A friend who was a bartender par excellence rushed over to me. "Want a beer?" she asked.

"No, thanks."

Another, a quintessential hostess, approached me next. "Do you know how to pick steamed crabs?"

"I sure do," I said.

I was the widow of a North Carolina coastal seafood eater, a man born and bred on the shores of Bogue Sound. Crab-pickin' became second nature for me when I married into Tim's family.

But my anxiety had risen to full throttle. "There are so many new people. I really don't know anyone," I said. "I think I'll go back home."

Just then my friend Marcia, one of the ladies who had visited me in Holly's darkest hospital days, hopped up and beckoned to me. There was an empty seat between her and a good-looking guy whom I had never seen before.

My first thought was, *Whoever that guy is, he is going to be really annoyed if I come between him and Marcia!* Marcia was, and is, a beautiful woman.

Reluctantly, I poured myself a glass of lemonade, sat down, and began a conversation with dear Marcia.

The guy on my right extended his hand to me and said, "I'm Kevin Brady."

"Oh, hi," I responded. "Terry Jones."

We shook hands, and I turned back to Marcia. But the guy was determined to engage me in conversation. He kept talking and talking to me until finally I gave up and listened. Marcia turned to the woman on her left for conversation. It wasn't long before I realized I was slightly mesmerized by this Kevin. After an hour or so, the tone of our tête-à-tête, which had focused on his fascinating experiences as a ship's master in the United States Merchant Marines, morphed into the personal realm.

"You're a very attractive woman."

"Thank you."

"About five foot four, a hundred and twenty pounds?"

"About right," I said with amusement.

"Any tattoos or body piercing?"

"Oh! You are a bold and flirtatious somebody!" I protested.

"Okay. I won't talk to you anymore."

"Fine with me," I said.

And we never stopped talking.

After more conversation, Kevin said, "Let's go in the kitchen. I want you to see my tattoo."

"Where is it?" I asked with apprehension.

"Right here," he said, pointing to his right deltoid.

As we pushed back our chairs, Marcia, ever the southern lady, inquired as sharply as if she were our chaperone, "Where are you two going?"

"To the kitchen, so he can show me his tattoo."

"Not without me, you're not!"

I was in safe hands with Marcia. The three of us trooped into the kitchen. Kevin pulled up his sleeve to reveal King Neptune, Roman god of the sea, permanently emblazoned on his upper arm.

"Tastefully done," I said, as I laughed and admired the green, blue, and crimson details of the tattoo.

"My mother thinks it's a work of art," he said.

His mother was the German lady with the French and Irish names, the one who had cried in the church narthex the morning of Holly's funeral. She'd brought him to the crab feast. He hadn't wanted to be there, either. Mama Renée had talked him into it.

In the kitchen after the tattoo display, I decided it was time to go home.

Kevin said, "I'll walk you out to your car."

Marcia looked nervous but didn't offer to escort us.

He opened the car door for me, and I got behind the wheel.

He leaned in and said, "I've made a new friend, but I don't think I should call you." He hesitated, and then gave me his card. "Here's my number, if you ever want to talk."

We smiled at each other, and waved goodbye.

What a nice guy, I thought as I drove home. *He's fun, and handsome, too.*

These were remarkable, unexpected thoughts for me to be having at that time in my life.

Twelve hours after I'd described my life of depression and loneliness in my journal, I wrote:

> *Something amazing has happened. I've met someone. Oh dear. I didn't expect this AT ALL. I don't know how to handle this "dating" thing. Oh, help! But thank You for letting me feel attractive again.*

It took me two full days to gather up the courage to call him. I don't know about love at first sight, but we were truly infatuated at first sight. He showed up at my house the following weekend bearing a bouquet of flowers and smiling nervously. We drove down the road for a barbecue sandwich. He kissed the back of my hand in the old-fashioned European manner.

Neither of us was a spring chicken. Kevin, in his early fifties, was several years younger than me. But together we behaved like teenagers. We held hands, talked incessantly on the phone, snuggled, and smooched.

~

Earlier that summer, I'd had a dream. I wrote it in my journal and forgot it for a while:

> *I fall in love with a strong handsome man, a sexy man. We kiss, standing up, amid a large group of people. Does he love me, too? Renée Brady is there, telling some of us at a table about her life in Nazi*

Germany as a child. I'm horrified, and wonder how anyone survived such ordeals. There is a huge fish tank, and a large fish is lowered into it. The fish will stay there and become acclimated and then be joined by others, and this will be a very good thing. But before that can happen, a tragedy occurs—the death of someone of local renown. I'm with a large group of people at an outdoor amphitheater where people are singing hymns and gathering, first as a standing congregation and then seated in perfectly arranged rows of chairs set in a semicircle. I wonder if the big fish is okay, and then I'm swimming in a clear pool, swimming right along with many fish. I no longer seek the approval of other women. I desperately seek union with the inner golden boy, the handsome Teutonic lover. How I desire that lovely man. But is he ready for me? Does he want me? Truthfully, though, I realize my responsibility is to care for the inhabitants of the unconscious, the fish, surfacing and making themselves known to me.

Although I've had dreams that come true about myself and about others, I don't ever know which ones will prove to be predictive. But this one most certainly foretold my future.

CHAPTER TWELVE

Then, through Faith

Sorrow lend me words, and words express
The manner of my pity-wanting pain.

—Shakespeare, Sonnet 140

Meeting Kevin was totally unexpected. My life changed almost overnight.

My husband, Tim, had been dead for sixteen months and fourteen days. There were times I really missed him. I missed talking to him, especially laughing with him. He had the ability to amuse me with his humor and insights, his wit and wisdom. I admired him, loved him, was passionate for him, and sometimes wanted to strangle him for his strange, moody ways.

I missed my daughters all the time, sometimes almost unbearably. I believe the grief of losing a child is the greatest grief imaginable, and inconceivable to one who has never experienced it. The parents of healthy children can only stare in breathless disbelief, wondering how such loss can be endured.

Yet my fractured heart wanted to embrace life, my life, the life I was given.

One day I was talking on the phone with a relative who had also lived through some tough times.

I said, "We have to live the hand we're dealt."

"Well, we sure weren't dealt winning hands," she snapped back, voice tinged with anger.

This startled me for a minute, until I realized that I did not see our situations that way. "I don't feel I've had a losing hand. A challenging and difficult hand, but not a losing one."

On the other end of the phone, there was a pause, and then I could hear surprise creep into her tone as she mused, "That's a good way of looking at it."

In my opinion, that's the only way of looking at it. Everyone suffers losses and setbacks at some time in life; loss is part of the human condition. How we respond to the events of our lives makes so much difference.

There's a word created from two Latin words by Hildegard von Bingen, the great twelfth-century mystic nun, who not until the twentieth century began to be recognized for her visionary gifts. The word is *veriditas,* from the Latin words for *green* and *truth.* Hildegard intended her new word to mean the divine life-giving force that imbues all of the natural and spiritual worlds.

Matthew Fox is a former Dominican priest silenced by the Vatican for such "heresies" as reawakening the West to the Christian mystical tradition. Now an Episcopal priest and founder of Wisdom University in Oakland, California, Fox wrote in his commentaries on the text of *Illuminations of Hildegard of Bingen:* "A dried-up person and dried-up culture lose their ability to create. This is why drying up is so grave a sin for Hildegard."

I believe that I'm proof positive that our hearts, with faith in God, can come back from the aridity of anguish, turning desolate deserts into fruitful gardens.

My empty life and my empty heart were ready for Kevin, because I had worked hard to understand the powerful force of a broken heart. There is power in the fractured heart when the torn-open broken places are attended with compassion.

~

Besides being a widow and bereaved mother living alone, my spine was twisted from arthritis, scoliosis, and spinal stenosis. In reaction to these conditions, the joints around the lumbar vertebrae had produced bone spurs, contributing to almost constant excruciating pain. One night I sat in the floor of the bathroom and sobbed. I wondered how I would live out my days in so much pain and all alone.

Since Tim's death, my spinal condition had deteriorated, and I had begun to recognize that part of the physical pain was an emotional reaction to a lifetime of serving as the scaffolding that propped up those around me. First, I was the responsible oldest sibling and protector of my younger sisters. After my marriage, I was the primary caregiver for my beautiful children, and the solitary support system for my needy husband.

I talked to my spine in my meditation times and when I woke up in pain in the middle of the night:

"All right, dear old spine. You've kept me upright and

going for all these years while I was the cheerleader for everyone else. Now you're demanding attention, and I'm going to give you the attention you crave. I don't want you to be screaming in outbursts of agony. You've served me well, and I hope that the two of us will be a mutually supportive team for two or three more decades. How can I give you comfort and relief?"

I believed that my back had kept everyone in my little family shored up for so long that it was tired of the demands placed upon it. My spine was protesting. It wanted to be honored with care and love.

"Thank you for giving me all these years of support. If I take better care of you, Spine, will the pain go away?"

After all the deaths were done, I hurt so badly that I finally went to a pain specialist for help. The x-rays at the physiatrist's office looked pretty scary. There was significant curvature in the lumbar region that I had previously seen on chiropractic x-rays, and the physiatrist also pointed out arthritis, bone spurs, and nerve damage. She sent me to the hospital for a myelogram, which was a terribly uncomfortable procedure. As he injected dye into the space surrounding my spinal cord, the radiologist, who was no doubt skilled in his field but lacked bedside manner, observed, "You have a twisted spine."

No kidding, I thought.

What, I wondered, was it like for my daughter Heather, at the age of three, to have a spinal tap? It was painful! No wonder she walked around our house all bent over like a tiny little old lady following that procedure. Now it was my turn. Was someone trying to show me what it was like to be my little daughters with their demanding physical conditions, that horrible disease that tried to dominate their lives but never dominated their spirits? There were times I feared my pain was getting the best of me.

I had chiropractic adjustments, massages, and acupuncture. I exercised. I took long walks. I went to Aquacize classes and did the Fitlinxx circuit at the Y. In fact, it was during a period of regular workouts at the Y that this terrible pain became acute, worsening in intensity. The pain turned nonstop and piercing; it would have been unbearable without pain medication, which merely took the edge off. Doctors prescribed Vicodin, Soma, Neurontin, and Percocet. They gave me Xanax and Tylenol III. I woke up with headaches from my drugged sleep. I slept on ice packs. I submitted myself to strenuous physical therapy sessions that didn't work.

One day I had a conversation with myself in the midst of the back pain and debility that I was experiencing, in the midst of the heavy headaches from drug combinations, in the midst of depression and loneliness and fretting.

Suddenly I asked myself, "Where is my head? Where is my heart? Is the locus of all my attentions in my lumbar spine? Oh, help! HELP!! I can't go on like this! I can't even work in my garden!"

And the answer I gave myself was, "Stop worrying about what you can't do, and get busy doing what you *can* do!"

Excellent advice, I thought, *and I shall follow it.*

Somewhere along the way in my lifetime of heartbreaks, that old admonition to become better, not bitter, in the aftermath of adversity had taken seed and sprouted in my consciousness. That's why I tell you some of these stories about my life. I tell you because I know you also can *be better not bitter,* in spite of whatever tragedies life may have hurled your way.

Finally, a breakthrough came. I heard about neuromuscular therapy, and I drove thirty-five miles to Virginia Beach in late-afternoon rush hour traffic where a neuromuscular therapist pummeled my sore deep muscles and smoothed out the tightened, constricted fascia. She tugged on my hair at specific areas of my scalp and energetic impulses shot into and out of my pelvic area and legs. It is amazing how body parts relate to other seemingly disparate parts. I had already conjectured that my spine was crumbling under the weight of too much heartache. I was pleased that my theory was given credibility in the alternative medicine field. It was liberating to know that bodily affliction had a direct correlation to the pains and grief that my heart had suffered.

The neuromuscular therapist said, "Everything is psychosomatic, because everything involves brain and body."

She did not mention heart, but that's part of it, as well, as are the energy centers, seven focal points of life force from the base of the spine to the crown of the head known as chakras. The whole organism is so complex and structured. Nothing is random. Everything is interrelated and connecting. For some time, I'd been nursing an interest in energy medicine and the study of the body's energy fields. I had taken classes in Healing Touch, a modality that works exclusively in the energy fields, and I'd experienced its remarkable benefits. I practiced Kripalu and Hatha Yoga, worked with chakra meditation, had massage therapy and Reiki treatments. I believe absolutely in the need for attention to the energy spheres in any healing process, but I definitely don't discount traditional medicine.

While I was undergoing the trials and tribulations of my life, I'd lost touch with my body's messages. Living in the oxymoron of chronic crisis as I did, I simply never allowed myself to relax. Understanding that the pains, diseases, and disabilities were part of the pattern of my lifestyle relieved my fear. It allowed me to nurture myself in a way that had been foreign to me.

~

Then along came Kevin, like a bolt out of the blue! We were like two lightning streaks, full of energy and excitement. We collided, and it was spectacular to experience. I hadn't realized it, but I needed Kevin to awaken my senses and fill me with joy.

I had fallen in love with him in my dream, months before I met him.

"You fill up my senses, like a night in the forest," sang John Denver in "Annie's Song." This song became our song, Kevin's and mine.

Kevin filled my senses in so many ways. He talked to me, and I was entranced. He listened to me, held me when I cried, and I was safe. In the beginning, there was the sexual connection. I was so attracted to him, right from the night we met. He leaned so close to me in the church parish hall, and his masculinity was all over me, penetrating my barriers, piercing my memory and the cells of my body with focused energy, potency, and vigor. Responding to him could not be put off, dismissed, or deferred. I was like a ripe fruit, needing to be plucked from the tree, needing to share myself and all that I had become. The physical intensity of our relationship was such that I feared we would burn out, be consumed in the fiery flames of our intense, fierce passion. Thrust toward one another by some arm of fate, we were insatiable.

We were playing our own adaptation of *Jeopardy* one evening when a small incident occurred that seemed to be the icing on the cake. In our version of *Jeopardy,* one of us would come up with a silly, simple clue, like "It's blue," and wait for the other to ask, "What is the sky?"

"Good guess but wrong!" the one giving the clue would say. "The answer is 'What is a moon over Kentucky?'"

Certain that I wouldn't know, Kevin said, "He wrote *Narcissus and Goldmund.*" Ha, you devilish little rascal, you cute little frisky Kevin. "Who is Hermann Hesse?" came my triumphant response. He looked at me, astonished. Hermann Hesse! This was an omen. Hermann Hesse, who was one of my very favorite authors and also one of my inner writing mentors, had been a friend and correspondent of Kevin's grandmother, his German Omi. Adding to our mysterious connectedness, his Irish grandmother had been Miss Terry before she married Mr. Brady.

This was uncanny, we believed, early in our relationship. We still do. The Universe plotted, planned, and coordinated something we could not ignore. Much of our early relationship was defined and informed by bliss, and we were deeply aware of a mystical communion, the spirituality of sexual ecstasy experienced by lovers who connect at a soul level.

The rebirth of a life from the ashes of an old one would not have been possible if I had not done the intense work of grieving for my lost life and loves. I sought help from support groups and from individual psychotherapy with a Jungian analyst. I read, journaled, and meditated. I prayed and cried. I worked very hard at becoming *better not bitter* in response to the tragedies and traumas of my life.

Like the mythical Psyche searching for her lost love

Eros, I was compelled to traverse the underworld faced with seemingly insurmountable challenges. And, just as Persephone counseled Psyche in the underworld, perhaps my earlier adventures with the Demeter/Persephone myth helped to bring me to a point at which I could rise from the ashes of my previous life.

Faith sustained me through the darkest of times. Grace made its presence known when I was ready to accept it. Even when I sat sobbing on the bathroom floor in the middle of the night, God was always there.

CHAPTER THIRTEEN

Summer

Now is the winter of our discontent
Made glorious summer. . . .
And all the clouds that lowered upon our house
In the deep bosom of the ocean buried.

—*The Tragedy of King Richard the Third,* act 1, scene 1

Kevin proposed to me. On bended knee, he took my hand, looked lovingly into my eyes, and asked, "Will you marry me?"

"Yes! Oh, yes I will!"

We were in the driveway. I'd just pulled up in my car, home from work. We could hear Creedence Clearwater Revival singing "Proud Mary" on the garage radio. Kevin slipped a square-cut diamond ring in an antique setting on my finger.

"You are the woman I've waited for my whole life," he said.

A thrilling moment! We hugged for a long happy time there in the driveway, hidden by trees from any prying eyes. Then we prepared a celebratory dinner. Crab had to be on the menu. We made crab au gratin with sautéed Brussels sprouts and drank champagne.

Proudly, I showed off my engagement ring at work, at church, and anywhere else I found myself.

Holly's best friend Stacie and her mother announced, "We're going to have a shower for you."

"Oh my goodness," I said. "I'm old. I was married for thirty-three years the first time around. I don't need a shower."

"We're going to give you a lingerie shower," they insisted. "We're going to fix you up."

"Oh. All right, then."

So one evening in early July, when the air was warm and fragrant with gardenias and roses, the mother and daughter pair hosted a lingerie shower for me. Stacie's house was filled with smiling, cheery ladies dressed in cool, feminine summer dresses. Festively wrapped packages displaying the Victoria's Secret logo piled high around me as I sat in the "chair of honor."

This is wonderful fun, I thought.

Sitting right next to me was an adorable white teddy bear wearing a purple hat and a purple rose. Definitely a female teddy, she played the Lennon/McCartney song "I Will" when a little button on her right front paw was pressed. A beautiful dress for the upcoming wedding, carefully sought after in store after store during shopping trips by myself and with a friend, hung in its plastic garment bag amid the clutter of my closet.

The ladies gave me flowered nightgowns, glamorous negligee sets, skimpy pajamas, and a bottle of bubbly.

I loved the role of bride-to-be!

My sister and her daughter and grandchildren flew from California to be with us for the wedding.

A few days after the lingerie shower, most of those same ladies and a few others were guests at a midday gathering given in my honor at another friend's perfectly appointed Smithfield home, overlooking the James River and the Gatling Pointe Country Club. Lillian's table offered all the delicacies of a southern lady's bridal luncheon—chicken salad with walnuts in tomato cups, deviled eggs, little pimento cheese sandwiches, watermelon pickles, marinated mushrooms, peach halves with cottage cheese topped with maraschino cherries, and ham biscuits.

Before lunch, the guests were offered stemmed crystal glasses of Mimosa cocktails, peach or raspberry.

A luncheon the likes of which my mother and grandmother would be proud, I mused to myself as I sipped a raspberry Mimosa.

Finally our big day arrived! The wedding of two people in late middle age who were deeply in love.

My handsome groom and I were joined in a fairytale ceremony at our tiny, historic, colonial Episcopal church. The church was packed with friends, well-wishers, and fellow worshipers; the day brought bright July sunshine and the miracle of low humidity in the southeastern Virginia summertime. Tim's brother, Don, escorted me down the aisle to Kevin as the congregation sang "Morning Has Broken."

The service was sacred and meaningful, planned by the two of us (broad-minded, eclectic Truth-seekers) and the officiating priest (proper Cambridge-educated British Anglican.) My youngest sister and Kevin's youngest brother stood with us. Kevin's mother read the scripture lessons in her well-modulated, German-accented voice. Our marriage was warmly, festively, and fondly celebrated.

Photographs show a joyous couple. The dress I'd chosen was a 1920s-era flowing celadon green, and Kevin wore a dashing suit with a coordinating celadon green shirt. We hadn't planned the color scheme. The surprising synchronicity was another sure sign to us that our union was meant to be.

Following the ceremony, a flawlessly catered brunch, complete with champagne punch and cascading cake, capped off the celebration. We danced, toasted each other, threw the bouquet and the garter. Making the merriment complete, we rode off into the warm midday sun on Kevin's Harley-Davidson, as guests laughed and threw birdseed.

An oil painting of our special day, presented as a wedding gift by acclaimed folk artist Kacey Carneal, hangs in our home. Kacey is the artist whose paintings had caught my eye in the lobby of the UVA Medical Center the day before Holly died. I'd later met her at a gallery opening that featured her works, and we became friends.

Kevin and I spent our honeymoon in a cottage at a bed-and-breakfast on the Pagan River in Smithfield, Virginia. We had a sitting area in front of a stone fireplace, a little kitchen where we partook of goodies from the picnic basket the caterer had prepared for us, a large bathroom with a great Jacuzzi, and a bedroom. Our cottage faced the river in one direction and a swimming pool in the other. We had the pool all to ourselves, and we romped and played like teenagers. The frolicking and the champagne went on into the night, splendidly.

On our wedding night I began to sing an old Frank Sinatra song: "Fairy tales can come true, it can happen to you if you're young at heart."

Kevin, whose taste in music runs to the Rolling Stones and Jimi Hendrix, planted a firm kiss on my lips so I had to stop singing. We laughed.

Then, as I continued to sing portions of the song, Kevin would interrupt with more kisses, more hilarity. Until finally, he could take no more. A huge kiss! I collapsed in laughter. It was fantastic to lie in bed with the man I loved and actually laugh out loud! How many times had lovemaking with Tim led to sad tears? No more! No more is sorrow the defining factor in my life.

I fell asleep with Kevin's arms around me, contented, comfortable, and happy.

~

Kevin calls my daughters "his girls." And truly they are his stepdaughters, even though he never met them. We remember their birthdays and commemorate their lives by placing flowers on the altar at church in their memory. Always he comforts me and then reminds me of our lives now, today. Our happy lives, our joy, our miracle in finding each other.

A friend told me shortly after my second daughter's death that Holly had said to her, "I want my mother to be happy."

I can't help but wonder. Do our deceased loved ones have an influence on our lives on earth? Did they bring Kevin and me together?

What I do know is this. I'm happy now because I had faith that somewhere within all the illness, death, and sorrow, there was God. I knew that I had no choice but to turn toward the Light of God.

~

Soon after Kevin and I met, he told me, "When I first walked up to your front door, I thought, 'Wow, she needs some help!' I mean, your yard was an overgrown mess."

My front yard was nothing but ivy, a whole lot of ivy growing under the trees and between the trees and the house. A whole yard full of ivy had grown from one small potted plant I'd put in the yard years before. Actually, I rather liked the ivy. It was green and required no work once it was established. It just kept growing and going.

But Kevin convinced me we needed to upgrade the landscaping. He pulled all the ivy out by the roots from two large areas, enough to make two gorgeous big flowerbeds. They're established now, splendid in spring, summer, and fall. I love watching green shoots pop up from the drab winter ground every spring. As I walk past the shade garden in midsummer, I notice how some of the plants—gingers, astilbes, hostas, hydrangeas, and ferns—lean toward the sun even though they're shade lovers.

That's what I did. I turned toward the light. Not to do so would have meant burrowing deeply into the *winter of discontent* and staying there in bleak despair. I paid attention to my inner voice. Through faith, I turned toward God's light. God's grace gave me a new love and a new life.

Kevin and I are happy together, living quietly through all the seasons of the year, in the autumn of our lives.

CHAPTER FOURTEEN

Scared Witless

The course of true love never did run smooth.

—*A Midsummer Night's Dream,* act 1, scene 1

A shallow glass bowl sat on the table, filled with camellias that I'd picked before the snow fell. Mostly red, a few pink, the flowers were a counterpoint to the monochromatic scene I saw through the windows. Pristine snow draped the trees and carpeted the ground. The leaves of the beech trees, which turn brown in the autumn but wait until March to fall to the ground, poked through the snow like occasional punctuation marks. Fat ground-feeding juncos nibbled on seed we'd scattered in the snowy yard.

The wooly bear caterpillar's wide black stripes and the *Old Farmer's Almanac* were on the money this year with their forecast of a snowy winter. Kevin and I took a morning walk in the bright cold. Icy gnarls jutted out from tree trunks, and tiny hollies sprang up from the woodland floor. It was breathtakingly beautiful. We returned from our walk invigorated and ready for mugs of hot tea.

The day was calm. I was filled with contentment. Kevin watched *Goodfellas* for the umpteenth time. A chair in front of the fireplace beckoned to me, and I curled up with a book and enjoyed the flickering warmth. When the low winter sun began to set, I looked out the window and marveled at the peace and joy in my life. My happiness with Kevin and in our life together continued to amaze me.

A few nights after our idyllic winter weekend, Kevin complained of a stomachache and proceeded to heave up dinner. The following day, he told me he'd been having severe pains in his belly and had been constipated for three days. I gave him three Dulcolax tablets, which I happened to have on hand because we both had been required to take this laxative, along with others, for recent colonoscopies. He felt so sick that he went to bed, with lights out and the door closed, immediately after our light supper of soup and crackers. Unheard of—he had never done this in our eight years together. When I went into the bedroom to check on him, he said, "Thank you for loving me."

His voice was plaintive. This was not like Kevin, and it was worrisome to me.

"I do love you," I said.

"I know you do, and I love you, too, Honey. So much."

Downstairs, I noticed that the camellias in the glass bowl were fading. I left them where they were, still pretty despite turning brown around the edges.

In the morning, hurting, he went to see his primary care physician, an internal medicine specialist.

"This is the result of the colonoscopy two weeks ago. Part of your colon was nicked. You are exactly in the time-frame for nausea, pain, and vomiting following that event," said the doctor.

The next afternoon, Kevin had a fever. Soon he began to moan. By evening he was almost screaming. Mr. Macho, who usually hid pain, sounded like a woman in labor. I almost couldn't bear to see him like that. We raced to the ER at Harbour View, where he was given an injection of morphine and put through an assortment of blood tests, x-rays, and ultrasounds. The morphine wore off quickly, and the nurse injected Dilaudid, then more Dilaudid thirty minutes later. He received a total of six injections of morphine or Dilaudid during three hours in the ER.

The diagnosis was gallstones. The ER doctor said Kevin had all the classic symptoms of a gall bladder attack. He wrote a prescription for Vicodin and told us to call a general surgeon in the morning. He gave us the surgeon's name and number. I took Kevin home, then dashed to the pharmacy for the Vicodin. We made it through the night. The next day was Friday, February 5.

I called the surgeon's office. A computerized answering system responded, listing upwards of ten menu choices. I pressed the number that sounded most likely to be the right one for reaching an appointment-making person, and got another voice-mail. I left a detailed message for a woman named Linda and asked her to please call me as soon as possible. She didn't. Kevin was hurting badly.

Kevin's primary care physician had received a report from the ER via computer, and phoned us. Kevin told him we hadn't been able to get in touch with the surgeon's office.

Kevin's doctor said, "I'll call them."

Soon he called back. "You may have to wait, but they've squeezed you in for a twelve forty-five appointment."

We were on our way to the surgeon's office at the Harbour View Health Center. I was driving, and Kevin was clutching his belly when his cell phone rang. It was the surgeon's nurse.

"Dr. M has been called out on an emergency and can't see you today."

I made a U-turn and headed back home. We were both getting irritated.

Kevin called his PCP, who made him an emergency appointment with a gastroenterologist. Back in the car, we headed toward Harbour View again. He was called in—quickly this time—to see a gastroenterologist, an associate of the physician who did the colonoscopy.

The GI doctor agreed with the gallstones diagnosis and said that Kevin also had diverticulitis. He arranged for Kevin to be seen immediately in the ER by a surgeon, but not the one we had tried to contact. We walked next door to the Harbour View emergency department where the receptionist was expecting us. We were ushered into a little room where a nurse, who seemed to be in the manic phase of a bipolar episode, examined Kevin. The nurse bounced around and talked very fast, asking one question after another, rapid fire, and cracking jokes. He told us about his mission trip to Africa on board a Mercy Ship. He was quite entertaining, and for the first time in three days, Kevin and I smiled.

Soon the surgeon who had been in the OR showed up wearing his green scrubs and puffy hat that looked like a shower cap. Above thick glasses, his dark eyes were kind.

He examined Kevin and said, "Your gall bladder must come out. We will do the surgery on Monday morning, and you'll go home the same day. Have nothing solid to eat until then. I will give you Percocet for pain, and Cipro and Flagyl to fight infection during the weekend. My office will call you to schedule the surgery." He shook hands with both of us and looked me directly in the eye. His compassion was almost palpable.

Outside it had started to snow again. I got behind the wheel of Kevin's vehicle, which we were in because it has four-wheel drive and the day was wintry. On a busy road on the way home, the windshield wiper on the driver's side stuck. I was driving with my neck craned around to the passenger side as the snow fell harder. My anxiety level rose dramatically, but we made it home safely.

Another run to the pharmacy, the second this week, and I was back again with the new prescriptions. Kevin took the Cipro, a powerful antibiotic that my daughter Holly took routinely and with no problems, to ward off bacterial infections. He took the Flagyl, along with pain medication. By Saturday afternoon, February 6, Kevin's fever was spiking, and he had turned into a grump.

A friendly lady, whose Asian accent made her a little hard to understand over the phone, called and told us the surgery would be at Chesapeake General Hospital.

"I will call you back to let you know of the time."

Later Saturday, we heard from her: "You must go to Our Lady of Prompt Succor instead of Chesapeake General."

That's better, we thought, a little closer to home.

Again she said, "I will call you later with the time."

Between the fever spikes, which occurred at regular intervals through the weekend, Kevin was hungry. He ate the broth that I prepared for him and drank a lot of juice and tea. He was cranky, and I was getting that way, too. He snapped at me and grumbled at the dogs. I tried to be understanding and patient. By Sunday night we were both anxious about Monday morning. We hadn't heard when to be there. Finally, around eight o'clock, someone called and told us to be at Our Lady of Prompt Succor at five a.m.

"Nothing to eat or drink after midnight. Do not take your medications in the morning."

Monday morning, February 8, we were on the road at four fifteen and at the hospital's front door at five. Another couple, sitting in their car, called out to us, "The sign says they don't open until five thirty."

But Kevin tried the door and it opened, and we all gave one another thumbs up. The lobby was deserted. A sign said, "Dial 4200 if you are here for outpatient surgery." Kevin followed instructions, and a voice on the other end of the line said, "Come up to the second floor, surgery waiting room." Again we followed instructions. We walked into an unoccupied waiting area with twenty chairs in varying rows around the room, an unattended reception desk, and an empty coffee pot. A large flat-screen TV hung on the wall, tuned to a local station that repeatedly gave us the traffic report for the morning, as well as the day's weather report.

Soon the couple we'd met at the front door trudged into the waiting area. They were large people, both of them. He was clearly the patient. He walked with a cane and carried a suitcase. She munched potato chips and sipped a coke. The man was cheerful and friendly. "It's a blessed day," he said with a smile.

As other patients and their families entered the room, he greeted each one, "Good morning! Have a blessed day."

One woman, overweight and accompanied by her overweight daughter, snarled back, "What's good about it?"

We soon discovered that it was a day when a number of gastric bypass surgeries were scheduled.

At six twenty, a nurse came out to get Kevin. "We'll come get you in a little while," she told me. And soon she came for me, and took me into the pre-op area where Kevin lay on a gurney wearing a hospital gown. His IV was in place. I squeezed into a chair in the tiny cubicle, trying not to push through the curtain into our neighbor's space. There was much bustling about and chattering in the unit.

"This is a busy place," I said to one of the nurses who came in to take Kevin's blood pressure.

"Several surgeries are scheduled for seven. Things will quiet down soon."

One by one, we watched as patients were wheeled out of pre-op. The anesthesiologist came in, told Kevin to say, "Aaah" and observed, "Your mouth is dry."

"You guys won't let me have a drink of water," said Kevin.

We heard someone say, "Dr. S just called. He's on his way."

A few minutes went by, and then Dr. S, the surgeon, pushed back the curtain to our partition. Wearing a black turtleneck and a beret, he looked like he stepped out of *A Moveable Feast,* like maybe he was an ex-pat in 1920s Paris.

Kevin asked, "Where were you at five o'clock?"

Dr. S grinned, looked at me, and said, "I like him." He went back out through the curtains.

Finally, with the pre-op unit quiet, since Kevin was the last patient left, they wheeled him away. I gathered our belongings and returned to the surgery waiting area where I poured myself some coffee and sat down to work the day's crossword puzzle. I'd brought along Sunday's puzzle, too, in case the waiting time was longer than expected. Monday's crossword is always quick and easy.

Doctors in scrubs began ambling in, telling other patients' loved ones that their mothers/sisters/husbands were doing very well. I was getting restless. I went to the vending machine in the hall and bought a bottle of water and some crackers. I opened the book I'd brought just in case the crosswords didn't take up the time.

Finally I saw Dr. S. He paused a moment and said, "Let's step out of the room."

We walked into the hallway between the waiting area and the operating rooms.

He looked at me with his kind eyes and said, "I am going to admit him for observation overnight. There is some internal bleeding that we didn't expect."

He handed me a photograph of Kevin's gall bladder and pointed out the stones. I felt faint. Not because of the gall bladder picture, but because Kevin was being admitted to the hospital. My eyes filled with tears. Dr. S patted me on the shoulder. "We will let you know when he's in a room," he said.

Sitting in the waiting room again, I started to weep. The granddaughter of one of the gastric bypass patients put her arm around me and said, "You don't need to be alone."

I thanked her and composed myself. I called a couple of close friends. I cried some more.

After what seemed like a long time, someone took me up to the fifth floor, the unit where Kevin had been transferred. He looked just awful. He was hooked up to an IV pole and his face was pale and waxy. Kevin is a muscular, physical guy. Early in our relationship, I'd once grabbed his bicep and joked, "Don't you ever lose those muscles, understand me?"

But in the hospital bed, he looked frail. I was scared.

At lunchtime Dr. N, his internist, came in and told me Kevin probably had pancreatitis.

All right, I thought. *We have a diagnosis, and where there's a diagnosis, there's a treatment.*

Later we saw a GI doctor, an associate of the one who had said a few days ago that Kevin had diverticulitis. This one, Dr. L, said, "I really don't know why they've kept you. And I don't believe you have diverticulitis because your pain was in a different quadrant of the abdomen from where we usually see the diverticula flare up."

When my daughters were undergoing hospitalizations, the medical staff functioned as a team. Here, it seemed as if each physician acted autonomously, and the overworked nurses were clueless. *Does the right hand know what the left hand is doing?* I wondered.

I stayed with Kevin until eight thirty that night. He was uncomfortable and cross. I was tired and worried. I kissed him goodbye and headed home, knowing I'd have to clean up doggie messes. Our sweet dogs had been confined to the house for sixteen hours. They'd be hungry and most likely feeling abandoned.

In our kitchen, I hugged my dogs, whose tails were wagging vigorously. I fed them. After a hot bath and some Tension Tamer Tea, I went to bed and fell asleep, exhausted. At twelve thirty a.m., the phone woke me up. Dr. N was calling.

"I am moving your husband to ICU. His fever has gone very high, and his blood pressure is eighty over fifty. We need to watch him closely."

I didn't go back to sleep. Wandering around the house, I noticed that my lovely camellias had dried up, and I threw the brown things into the trash. Weeping, I crawled back under the covers and waited for the sun to rise in the February sky.

Toward dawn, I dozed. When the dogs woke me up to start the day, I remembered that my world had suddenly gone topsy-turvy. I called the nurses' station on the fifth floor. "He's still in ICU," someone told me, and transferred my call. Kevin's ICU nurse told me in broken English that Kevin had had a restless night, but they were preparing to transfer him back to the floor.

A mist of numbness tried to settle itself around me, but the prickly raw pain refused to be covered up. I tended to our dogs. They were Meggie, our senile Dachshund; Celine, our aging Brittany spaniel; and Mia, our youngest, a rescued English bulldog. I drifted aimlessly around the house; forced myself to get dressed. Should I have breakfast? Or had I had breakfast? I didn't think so. There was an empty space inside me somewhere. I ate a bowl of cereal and drank lots of coffee.

At the information desk in the hospital lobby, I inquired as to the whereabouts of Kevin Brady.

The lady checked her computer. "He's in surgical intensive care."

"Still there?" I was dismayed. The lady looked sympathetic.

"I can go up there, can't I?" I felt bewildered, lost and alone.

Still with her sympathetic half-smile, she nodded.

I located the ICU and followed the requisite procedure for entering: dialing in, identifying myself. I discovered that Kevin's nurse was named Ernesto. He took me to a corner area, not even a cubicle. Behind a curtain, Kevin lay on his side in a narrow bed in an utterly impersonal place. There was a hard plastic chair where I put my things. He was hooked up to IVs. He didn't seem happy to see me, and that was baffling.

"How are you?" I asked.

"Miserable. Shuffled back here, cast aside."

"You're in intensive care, where you can get more attention."

"Bullshit. No attention. None. No sleep. People scream all night. I'm in prison."

His voice was a mumbled monotone. He wouldn't look at me. He was visibly despondent.

A patient, I supposed one who had screamed last night, was still screaming. My mind reeled against the surrealism of the surroundings.

Kevin said, "This place is filthy and moldy."

"Where?"

He pointed to the ceiling, to a heating duct.

"The vent is rusted," I said.

Ernesto walked in. "Soon you are going to the fifth floor."

"Am I going in this bed?"

"No. Transport will wheel you up."

Soon Transport arrived in the person of a husky uniformed woman. Had we been transported to *One Flew Over the Cuckoo's Nest*?

Ernesto and Transport loaded Kevin into a wheelchair. They attached his IV drip bag to the appropriate gadget on the chair, put his medical chart in its allotted slot, and covered his legs with a blanket. They plopped the bag filled with his personal belongings—shoes, jacket, jeans, and shirt—onto his lap.

When we arrived at the room newly assigned to Kevin, his nurse Alfredo met us. In excellent English, Alfredo told me to wait at the end of the hall while he did his nursing assessment. I followed instructions. Through a window, the drabness of the day matched my mood. Gray sky. The days-old snow on the ground and along the sidewalks was no longer pretty, but had turned slushy in spots and was dirty from street debris. When Alfredo beckoned, I returned to the room.

"Are you Kevin's nurse for the rest of the day?" I asked. I craved consistency, a familiar face.

"Another nurse is coming in—Loretta. Our census is high, and we need help."

Loretta arrived shortly, wearing a white nurse's uniform—a dress, white stockings, sturdy white shoes. Most of the nurses wore scrubs with solid color bottoms and tops printed with cheerful little butterflies, flowers, teddy bears, frogs, or even smiley faces. Not that wearing a white uniform would affect a nurse's skills one way or another. Just that it was rare and seemed more formal.

"You must be the new hire," said Kevin. There was a little edge in his voice.

I thought, *Good, he's getting some of his spunkiness back.*

"I'm the agency nurse, in for the evening."

Loretta darted about, noticed the pneumatic compression stockings sitting on a chair. "You should have these on."

She hooked them up, and I realized they were the same devices Holly wore when she was in a medically induced coma following her transplant. I called them her moon-walking space boots. In fact, they were mechanical leg pumps intended to prevent painful, potentially fatal blood clots.

The fog of numbness began to creep around me again. The shroud that protected me and helped me survive years of my daughters' chronic illnesses was trying to shelter me now. When the girls were sick, I had a role. Uselessness seemed to be the only part I played in this turmoil, and I was not accustomed to being useless.

The recliner in the room was old but a huge upgrade from the hard plastic chair that had been next to Kevin's ICU bed. I sat and opened my book at the bookmark. The book was Greg Mortenson's *Stones into Schools.* Offhandedly, I wondered if Dr. N would notice that the cover of the book showed five little girls, black hair peeking out from Muslim headwear, against a barren backdrop of hilly desert. Dr. N was from the Middle East. He trained in internal medicine in London, Egypt, and Virginia. He had been Kevin's primary care physician for several years, and Kevin had much respect for him.

Kevin complained of being very cold. I covered him with an extra blanket. A nurse's aide took his temperature a while later; it was higher than earlier, though not as high as last night. Dr N walked into the room wearing an elegant black overcoat and scarf. He was standing near the door, observing Kevin, when Loretta scurried in with medicine cups and some water.

"Why are you giving him oral medication?" Dr. N asked.

"It's the Cipro and the Flagyl."

"He is to have that by the IV."

"This is what pharmacy sent up."

"That's wrong. Let's go look at the chart together."

She gathered up the unadministered medication, looked frustrated, and left the room with the doctor. Through a fog, my brain queried, "Why the confusion?"

Kevin grumbled, "Probably nothing but snake oil."

Dr. N returned. "Dr. S changed the order from IV to oral."

"So. He overruled you," said Kevin.

"No. He overruled himself. No one overrules me." He grinned. "I've changed it back to IV infusion."

He placed his stethoscope on various parts of Kevin's abdominal area.

"Another night or so, and we'll send you home."

Supper trays were distributed. Kevin picked at some orange Jell-O and brown broth. The trays were collected, then Kevin's brother Blake came to visit. He wore camouflage pants and a fleece jacket, still zipped up tight against the cold wind in the parking lot.

"Why'd they put you in this place?"

Twelve years earlier, their father had been admitted to Prompt Succor and while there, suffered a stroke and died. None of the three brothers had kind things to say about Our Lady of Prompt Demise Hospital, as the local population often calls it, and I imagined it was about to get worse.

On Wednesday morning, I was still in my pajamas as I stared out the window at our winter-bare gardens with their skeletal promise of spring buds and summer flowers. I missed Kevin terribly. I felt so sad. Tears stung my eyes. The phone jangled.

"Hello?"

"Good morning, Mrs. Brady," came Dr. N's high-timbre singsong voice. "I have some questions to ask you."

"Okay."

"Does Kevin drink?"

"He enjoys a beer most evenings after work, and wine occasionally. He doesn't get drunk."

"And something else. . . . I don't want to offend you."

"Go ahead."

"Does he use drugs? Marijuana?"

"I'm sure he has smoked marijuana in the past," I said. But I was thinking, *Kevin had hair down to his waist back in the day, and he went to Woodstock. Of course he smoked pot in his younger days.*

"Because he is confused sometimes. I will have a neurologist look at him."

"Okay," I said. "By the way, you mentioned pancreatitis the other day. What about that?"

"We have ruled out pancreatitis. And, Mrs. Brady, any time you have a question, please feel free to call me. If it is after office hours, call the answering service and tell them to page me."

"Thank you."

Later that morning, a doctor in a white lab coat walked into the hospital room. He sported a mustache and goatee. Dr. Freud, I presume?

He introduced himself. "I'm a neurologist, and I study brains."

He sat down and began a casual conversation with Kevin. They chatted about movies, about Kevin's career as a ship's master in the United States Merchant Marines, and about the *Exxon Valdez.* Then the neurologist asked him, "What day is it today?

"The tenth of February."

"Who is the president of the United States?"

"Barack Obama."

"Your brain is fine."

He turned to me. "The mental confusion correlates with spikes in temperature, which are occurring at regular intervals. I'll show you on the chart."

We walked to the nurses' station, and he pointed to the graph of temperatures. It seemed that every six hours, Kevin's temperature went up, and that's when he got addled.

"When I was in medical school, I learned that fevers that spike at regular intervals are caused by abscesses. He has an abscess."

"Where is it?"

"I have no idea."

I felt relieved. I was certainly glad that Kevin didn't have an abscessed brain.

So far, he'd been treated by the following medical specialties: general surgery, gastroenterology, internal medicine, and neurology. What the heck? Would they try applying leeches next? I was frustrated, and I was scared. I observed the pattern: shaking chills, fever spikes, then delirium.

"Where are we?" Kevin asked me in the afternoon. "Is this a classroom?" He looked intently at a dry erase board, on which a nurse had written:

GOALS:
DECREASE FEVER
GO HOME

That day, his nurse was a tall woman named Kay, who gave him an injection of Atavan. Soon his confusion and agitation were gone, and he drifted into sleep. When he woke up, I noticed a dark red-brown lesion on his lip. Dr. N noticed it, too, when he made rounds in the evening.

"What's that?" he asked.

"I'm wondering the same thing. The neurologist told me he has an abscess which is causing the fever spikes."

He left the room, returned and reported, "He does not have an abscess."

Again, there was the stethoscope on the abdominal area and chest. Again, he said, "We need to keep you another night or so." And again he said to me, "Do not hesitate to call me if you have questions."

Later, I got ready to leave. "I love you," I said to Kevin.

"I wish I could say I love you, but I don't love anyone or anything. I want to kill myself."

Oh. My. God.

I knew this was fever, medication, and illness talking, but I got angry.

"Good night, Kevin."

At home, I cried. After a sleepless night, I called Dr. E, my psychiatrist. I'd been in touch with her since Monday morning, when the surgeon admitted Kevin for observation. She soothed me and told me that he was in a safe place (was he?). She said the not loving anyone and the suicide talk revealed his hopelessness and helplessness. She prescribed an anti-anxiety medication for me, which I gratefully agreed to take. I was an exhausted, useless, barely functioning basket case.

Thursday morning. Kevin was uncomfortable and grumpy. I was scared witless. I didn't understand why he didn't seem glad to see me when I got to the hospital each morning. When my daughters were hospitalized, they were always happy to see me. We took walks, pushing IV poles around the hospital corridors. We played cards and board games and watched movies together. Kevin had no interest in anything.

Another difference I'd noticed: at every admission to King's Daughters or the University of Virginia Medical Center, the girls were issued a little kit containing a toothbrush, toothpaste, mouthwash, lotion, and soap. And, they were provided with a pitcher of water and a plastic cup. At this hospital—nothing. I brought him a toothbrush, toothpaste, and a bar of soap. I had to ask repeatedly for a cup of water. Kevin was thirsty. The nurse apologized. "I'm sorry. I forgot."

They decided he was allergic to Cipro. They discontinued that and replaced it with Zosyn. He was still getting Flagyl. The sores spread all around his lips, and his skin looked yellow.

An infectious disease physician was called in. The fifth specialist. She diagnosed herpes simplex and added the antiviral medication Acyclovir to his drug smorgasbord. She ordered a chest x-ray and a scan of some sort.

At home that night, I wrote in my journal for the first time since this nightmare began:

> *I don't know if Kevin and I will get through this after all. Not together, anyway. It has been a horrible past three days, and seems much longer than that. I can't do it. I can't help him.*

Friday, February 12. The chest x-ray looked perfect. The scan showed nothing. The fever was going down. The surgeon and the GI doctor cleared him to go home. Infectious Disease didn't. Dr. N told Kevin, "If you remain fever-free for the next twenty-four hours, I will discharge you."

My journal entry early Saturday morning:

> *Snow here again today. Kevin is still in the hospital. Our Lady of Prompt Succor is too far away, too inconvenient, too old, and too understaffed. It may be that other hospitals are understaffed as well, but I've never had experience with a hospital that doesn't give a cup of water to its patients without begging and pleading on the part of the patient's wife. Never before have I seen Kevin depressed, and he seems very depressed to me now.*

I headed to the hospital with some clean clothes for him in the car, his going-home clothes. When I got to his room, he said, "You just missed Dr. N. I'm not leaving today."

Depression was giving way to resignation. I heard it in his voice. And he was even more yellow. He looked like the outside of a mustard jar. The whites of his eyes were now the yellows.

Yet another physician appeared in the doorway wearing green scrubs.

"I thought—I hoped—he would be discharged today," I said to Dr. Whoever-He-Was.

"We think his liver is failing. He could die."

I recalled again that this hospital is known sarcastically as Our Lady of Prompt Demise. The doctor listened to Kevin's belly and chest, smiled at me, and left the room.

I went to the desk and asked the unit clerk to please page Dr. N. If he was still in the hospital, I wanted to talk to him. I didn't understand what was going on, and I needed answers.

The phone at Kevin's bedside rang, and I picked up the receiver.

Dr. N said, "Mrs. Brady, you are very difficult."

"But you told me if his fever remained low for twenty-four hours that I could take him home."

"The infectious disease doctor will not allow me to discharge him. She thinks he has a brain infection."

"A what?"

"A *brain* infection. Did he tell you he refused to have his vitals taken last night?"

"He refused to have his temperature taken?"

Donna, his nurse for two days, had walked in and overheard my question. She shook her head. Kevin shook his head, too. I said, "Kevin and the nurse both are telling me he didn't refuse."

Dr. N yelled at me. "Are you calling me a liar? You are saying I am lying to you?"

"No. I'm saying I'm getting conflicting information."

"Then you are calling me a liar. Do you want another doctor to take my place?"

"I think you'd better talk to Kevin," I said. I handed the phone to him and asked Donna about the "refusal." She said, "I didn't hear anything about it in report this morning."

I asked her to find it in the chart. She showed me the notation made by the nurse aide last night at 2100: Pt asleep. Wakes up, asks to be left alone. No vitals taken.

Another nurse told me that the infectious disease doctor had diagnosed herpes-induced encephalitis.

"Now that, I could have understood. A *brain* infection is a little vague."

"Many doctors don't realize that patients and their families can be educated people."

No shit, Sherlock.

The infectious disease doctor ordered a spinal tap. The

guy who was to do the procedure examined Kevin and said, "I won't do it. He doesn't need a spinal tap."

I began to cry. I paced around the room angry and weeping all at once. "I hate this! I hate all of it!"

Kevin said, "Oh, honey, please don't cry. We'll be all right. This will be over eventually."

He sat up on the bed, and I sat down next to him. His arm was around me and my head was on his shoulder. I sobbed and sobbed. I hadn't cried so since the death of my younger daughter.

By the time I got home Saturday night, there was a message on the phone. Kevin's voice, pitiful and lonely, came through the machine. "Honey, I miss my dogs. Please put Mia on a short leash and bring her to the hospital tomorrow."

I was angry enough that I was willing to break whatever hospital rules existed, so I called Kevin's youngest brother, Patrick.

"In the morning, I'm going to take Mia to your house. After I set things up at Our Lady of Prompt Succor, I'll call you. Please bring her to the hospital." Patrick, who enjoys all things slightly underhanded, agreed.

The next morning was Sunday. Before I got there, Dr. N stopped by the hospital. He was contrite. "I want to start all over again. I don't like fighting. Is your wife still mad at me? Oh, incidentally, the brain infection was a misdiagnosis." Then, "I'm on my way to church."

"Good place to go," I said when Kevin related the conversation to me.

Kevin's nurse was Donna, who had witnessed the phone fight between Dr. N and me the day before.

"Donna," I said, "Kevin's brother is going to bring our dog up to see him."

"A small dog?"

"She's an English bulldog."

"Hmmm. Maybe you could take Kevin down to the lobby in a wheelchair."

So we did that, and Patrick brought Mia into the hospital lobby, which was pretty much empty. Kevin's eyes lit up when he saw Mia, and they played for a little while, but soon he became tired. I wheeled him back to his room and told Patrick to use the rear corridor to sneak Mia up.

We closed the door to the room and a nurse said, "If anyone asks, it's a therapy dog."

She brought a plastic basin of water for Mia.

Kevin's spirits visibly lifted as he played with his beloved dog. After an hour or so, a nurse said, "A couple of doctors are making rounds."

Uh-oh, no more confrontations, please. I told Patrick to take Mia home. Kevin told her goodbye, "I'll be home soon, sweetheart." They licked and kissed, licked and kissed and hugged.

Soon there was a tap on the door, and a portly gentleman we'd never seen before entered the room. The badge on his jacket announced that he was associated with Chesapeake General Hospital. Clearing his throat, he muttered, "I notice you're taking thyroid medicine. Why are you taking that?"

Kevin and I looked at each other, bewildered. What? What now?

"Oh, sorry, they've asked me to look at you. I'm an endocrinologist."

The sixth specialist.

Several weeks later, when Kevin went for a follow-up appointment in his office, the endocrinologist said, "I didn't think you'd ever leave the hospital."

No wonder the man looked glum and mumbled under his breath that Sunday at Our Lady of Prompt Succor Hospital.

After poking around Kevin's neck and throat and of course listening with the ubiquitous stethoscope, he left.

Another light tap on the door, and a gastroenterologist came in. He was the same guy who'd told Kevin he had diverticulitis, a diagnosis with which his colleagues disagreed. He sat down and said, "I've just read your chart and as far as I'm concerned, you can go home."

Kevin was very happy to hear that. "If you get me out of here, I'll build an altar and genuflect to you."

"Don't do that," said the doctor "I know what happened the last time they did that to a Jewish guy." Everyone chuckled.

He put his stethoscope to Kevin's abdomen and chest, smiled, nodded, and left the room.

By Sunday night, no discharge orders were written. The doctors still did not agree. The infectious disease specialist wanted to do yet another scan. A scan of what, we were not certain.

Monday morning, February 15. Dr. J, a gastroenterologist who had treated Kevin during his bout with hepatitis C several years ago, returned from a medical meeting in Vail, Colorado. During the hep C episode, Kevin had to inject himself with Interferon weekly for six months, after which he was pronounced free from the hepatitis virus.

"Please don't ever have surgery of any kind without consulting me first," said the doctor.

"Well, buddy, you were off skiing in Vail," said Kevin.

Dr. J smiled slightly.

"I've cancelled the scan," he said. "You don't need it. But I want to have some fluid drawn from around your liver."

The level of communication among the doctors continued to be at zero.

That afternoon, a technician wheeled him on a gurney downstairs to a treatment room. She set up a video monitor, and then a doctor on loan from a facility in Washington, DC, walked in. A chatty fellow, he mentioned that he was originally from Canada but works in the States now. Our Lady needed extra help, so they'd called him down here for a few days. Kevin asked him about the Canadian health system, and the doctor said, "It works very well, contrary to what you read in the U.S. press."

Observing the video screen, Dr. Canada said, "I really don't see any fluid."

Nevertheless, he pulled out a long needle and was preparing to insert it into the liver area when Dr. J showed up and (in jest) said, "Stick it to him good."

Everyone watched while a one-liter bottle filled up halfway with clear liquid. Dr. Canada said, "You're pretty lucky. I just pulled out four liters of fluid from a guy who's a chronic alcoholic with a cirrhotic liver."

Tuesday morning, February 16. Dr. N told Kevin, "You have two choices. You may stay here for ten more days, or you may go home with a PICC line." Cautious as usual, he went on to say, "With the PICC line, you could get an infection around your heart. It could be very dangerous."

Predictably willing to risk it, Kevin said, "I'll go home with the PICC line."

And so it was arranged that a Peripherally Inserted Central Catheter (PICC line) would be inserted into Kevin's upper arm and threaded through a vein to terminate in a large vessel near his heart.

Once again, he was wheeled down to the treatment area

where Dr. Canada said, "Hey, it's you again." This time the conversation during the procedure revolved around the Winter Olympics, then taking place in Dr. Canada's native land.

In the evening, a nurse from the home health agency came to the hospital to explain to us how to access the line, how to keep it sterile, and how often to administer the medication. She set up a computerized gadget, which was timed to release the anti-viral medication at regular intervals. It was housed in a zippered pouch on a shoulder strap that Kevin had to wear all the time. "My purse," he called it.

When it was time for meds, we were to hook him up to a bag of saline and a bag of medication and insert a tube into the port on his upper arm. Déjà vu. My daughter had been discharged from the hospital with PICC lines, PAS-Ports, and ordinary heparin-locked IVs. We could do this.

Wednesday morning, February 17. I arrived at the hospital, and Kevin sped around getting dressed and signing discharge papers. A nurse transported him in a wheelchair to the hospital's entry, while I went to get the car. He was one happy fellow to be leaving Our Lady of Prompt Succor.

We were together again, home at last. The course of treatment with the PICC line lasted ten days, and went smoothly. A nurse checked in periodically and was always on call, but after being taught the procedure, we were able to do it without a hitch.

Daily, I could see Kevin improving in health and strength, while I needed rest, rest, and more rest after the ordeal.

Kevin continues to hold Dr. N in high regard; they have an excellent rapport.

But if there is a next time, should we take the advice of a physician friend and use the services of that relatively new specialist, the hospitalist? Would a hospitalist provide a point of coordination? Less confusion? Better communication? Maybe so and maybe not. I hope there will never be a next time.

So far, so good. It has been almost two years, and Kevin has had no more serious health issues, nor have I. He needed to get home to me, where we can take good care of each other as we grow older together.

CHAPTER FIFTEEN

Kevin and Me

Sit by my side, and let the world slip,
we shall ne'er be younger.

—*The Taming of the Shrew,* induction, scene 2

November is not my favorite month. Before I met Kevin, I wanted to sleep through the entire month. November was the month of Heather's birthday and Holly's death day. Although I'm thankful for my many blessings, the Thanksgiving holiday has been difficult ever since Holly died on Thanksgiving Eve.

The first few Thanksgivings that Kevin and I were together, we stayed home and invited his mom and brother over for Thanksgiving dinner. A lot of work went into those holiday dinners. I wanted to impress my new mother-in-law, Renate. Four days of cleaning, three days of cooking, two days of decorating, then mom-in-law and brother-in-law sat down, had a cocktail, ate turkey with all the trimmings, had a slice of pumpkin pie, and offered to help with the dishes. When I declined their offer of help, they said, "Thanks for having us over," and left.

The last year that we did Thanksgiving dinner, mom-in-law's mind was slipping.

After dinner, she shook her finger at Kevin in a German motherism. "This lady is the best thing that ever happened to you, you understand me?"

I had just finished clearing dessert plates from the table.

Kevin said, "Yes, Ma. I know it very well."

Mother and brother gave us each a little hug and left for their home.

Clearly, my new husband's family was different from the vast extended clan I had joined when I married my late husband, Tim, many years ago. At the Jones's table, we lingered for hours after the turkey, collards, cornmeal dumplings, mashed potatoes, candied yams, cornbread, biscuits, relishes, cranberry sauce, stuffing, gravy, and sweet iced tea were consumed. Cousins, uncles, aunts, sisters, and brothers reminisced and exchanged stories of their childhood escapades. Laughter abounded, and soon everyone was at the dessert table for seconds of sweet potato pie, banana pudding, pecan pie, coconut cake, or a little taste of everything.

When Renate developed Alzheimer's and wouldn't have known a Thanksgiving celebration from Easter Sunday, we started our tradition of going off to a bed-and-breakfast for the weekend.

Most recently, St. Michaels on Maryland's Eastern Shore sounded appealing, and we found a bed-and-breakfast that allowed us to bring our English bulldog, Mia (the other two dogs having passed). We would never traumatize our sweet rescued bullie by boarding her. Where we go, she goes, as the saying goes.

Our drive across the Chesapeake Bay Bridge Tunnel and up the Eastern Shore was pleasant and sometimes amusing. In one small Virginia town, we saw a sign in front of a mom-and-pop convenience store right on the highway that read, "PAY YOUR BILL!" and boldly listed the names of five or six locals who apparently hadn't caught up their credit balances.

One section of the Shore offered a string of *tiendas* and *iglesias,* your choice of *Evangelico* or *Catolico.* Their migrant clientele must have moved on to Florida in quest of riper fields and seasonal crops, because the Hispanic establishments looked empty.

We traveled through farmland and tiny villages with modest, freshly painted houses, and encountered a minor traffic jam in Salisbury. Approaching St. Michaels, we noticed that the houses were no longer unassuming white frames, but mansions far from the road on the waterfront. Later we learned that Donald Rumsfeld and Dick Cheney—that guy with no heartbeat—have weekend spreads in the area, complete with helipads.

The town of St. Michaels is quaint and charming, its narrow streets lined with gingerbread houses converted to storefronts, bistros, art galleries, and inns. Our B&B was about a half mile out of the main section of town, and it was lovely. We had a first-floor room with a door that opened onto a back porch overlooking a grassy area where we could walk Mia. The high four-poster bed was beautifully carved and canopied. A fireplace, writing desk, wing chair, tiled bathroom, faux-but-tasteful Tiffany lamps, and a large flat-screen TV completed the amenities. Jewel-toned Waverly coverings adorned the comfortable bed, and matching Waverly window treatments trimmed the three windows. Cozy elegance; just what we needed.

We checked in with the innkeeper and his much younger Russian wife. After settling Mia in with her toys and a bowl of water, we set out to explore. Our plan had been to bicycle into town, but the damp cold air changed our minds, and we drove the brief distance.

"I wonder if the innkeeper's wife is a mail-order bride," said Kevin.

"Huh? Do they still have those?"

"I think they do."

"Wow."

We parked next to the Mariners' Museum, which was closed, and strolled along Main Street, poking into touristy boutiques. My favorite was A Wish Called Wanda. We spent so much time looking around in Wanda's shop that I felt obliged to make a purchase. Bought a couple of pretty glass and silver bracelets, even though I rarely wear bracelets. I'm an earring and necklace kind of gal.

Next, we drove up and down the side streets where there were many houses on the market. "For Sale" signs lined the streets one right after the other. Kevin had me hopping out of the car to pick up Realtors' brochures for picturesque restored old homes of varying sizes, all overpriced and definitely overtaxed.

We meandered along the waterfront, and he pointed out the Grand Banks yacht he wanted for Christmas. Oh, yeah.

Our innkeeper had recommended Ava's on Main Street as the current in-place for dinner.

Ava's sign said, "Pizzeria and Wine Bar."

Kevin said, "I don't want pizza."

"Me neither. Let's go in and see what else is on the menu."

They had a full dinner menu, so we were seated by the window and relaxed into the evening.

"This is sweet," my honey said as we ordered our meal.

Back at the B&B, Mia was excited to see us, and we prepared for an early bedtime. Kevin settled in to watch TV, while I read and Mia snored. Just like home.

The next morning, Thanksgiving Day, was gray and drizzly. In the breakfast area, two other guests sat on a sofa sipping coffee.

"I am Elsa," said a pretty young woman wearing large fuzzy bedroom slippers.

"And I am Soren," said her tall bespectacled companion, standing up to extend his hand.

They both spoke foreign-accented English.

"Where are you-all from?" I asked.

"I'm from Denmark," Elsa said. "Now I live in Dumfries."

"I'm from Sweden," Soren said. "Now I live in Reston."

Just then another couple appeared. He was short, walked with a cane, had a little paunch, and about six strands of hair sticking straight up from a bald head. She was chubby with long straight brown hair and reading glasses over which she peered at us.

Introductions were made. He was Gerald. We never did find out her name.

Gerald noticed Kevin's shirt with a Harley-Davidson logo and proceeded to pontificate on the cycling world. We were soon to discover that Gerald pontificated on any subject whatsoever.

"Are you a biker?" I inquired.

"No. I ride motorcycles."

"Oh, I see."

"There's a big difference between being a biker and riding a motorcycle. Harleys are crap anyway. I ride Hondas."

Bless his heart—Kevin just listened. This guy Gerald seemed to be a nutcase.

In answer to the usual get-acquainted questions, Gerald said, "I live in Pennsylvania. She lives in Little Rock. Her company transferred her to Arkansas, and I can't sell the house in P-A. Six months now. It's getting old."

Gerald's wife and I found ourselves at the coffee pot together, and I asked what kind of work she did that required her to move to Little Rock.

"Receivables," she said in a tiny voice.

I guess I looked quizzical. She expanded, "Accounts receivable."

"Ah, I see."

We sat down at a table set for the six of us. The Russian wife wore a chef's outfit and served a delicious fruit cup followed by Belgian waffles and bacon.

Breakfast table conversation consisted of Gerald holding forth on any topic that anyone else brought up.

Elsa worked for Ikea. Gerald was an expert on Scandinavian furniture.

Soren worked for Amtrak. Gerald knew exactly what's wrong with the rail system in the U.S. of A.

Kevin's mother was a WWII German war bride. Gerald understood every detail of the German psyche.

Kevin is a retired Merchant Marine. Gerald knew the facts about every hurricane ever to cross the Atlantic from Africa.

We noticed that when Gerald got up from the table, he didn't use his cane and walked perfectly well. We figured

Gerald's wife, who had not uttered a word, supported his "disability" with her accounts receivable clerk's salary.

Kevin and I, with Mia in the backseat, set out for our Thanksgiving Day adventure. The shops in St. Michaels were all closed. We drove through Easton, an equally picturesque, somewhat larger town, where the shops were also closed and a lot of real estate was also for sale. We drove up the peninsula, across the Knapps Narrows Bridge, and onto Tilghman Island. Tilghman seems more remote than it actually is; it seems to be one of the last remnants of old-time Eastern Shore fishing villages.

We continued on and came upon a small military installation right on the Chesapeake Bay.

"Probably Coast Guard," Kevin said.

We drove a bit farther and came to a B&B at the very tip of the island, where the Choptank River and the Chesapeake Bay merge. Curious, we drove onto the property and a friendly fellow bounded out to welcome us.

"You want a room?" he asked, chipper as can be.

"We're booked into another inn tonight, but yours looks interesting for another time."

He handed us a brochure about the inn, which told us it was run by innkeepers Bill and Johnnie.

"Are you Bill?" I asked.

"I'm Johnnie," he chirped. "Bill's over there with his mom and dad."

We saw a small group walking toward the inn.

"Jump on out," Johnnie invited. "I'll give you the grand tour. Bill and I bought this place last July, and we are *so excited* about it."

Kevin asked about the military installation down the road.

"Oh, that's a Naval research lab. Probably *tons* of CIA

stuff goes on there. And guess what? The bigwigs from DC met *right here* at this bed-and-breakfast to plan the first Gulf War! I'll show you the room later. Of course that was before Bill and I were here." He beamed.

Johnnie was a gregarious young man who clearly loved his role as innkeeper. We toured the cottages, those that weren't rented, and then the main house that consisted of three floors, the top an attic room with a sloped ceiling, available for just $120.00 a night.

"We're smack dab in the middle of a bird sanctuary, and we also want to be a people sanctuary. So—if you ever find yourself in grief or trouble, just give us a call. We'll give you a discount and take good care of you. We'll nurture you through a divorce, a death in the family, any kind of difficulty you may find yourself experiencing."

He pointed to a huge cross on the shoreline and told us it had washed up on the beach, and they'd installed it in concrete.

He ushered us through the house and into the kitchen, with a "watch your step" at every doorway. Bill's mother, a sweet-natured plump lady whose red hair was fading to gray, and Bill's father, tall and thin, greeted us warmly. Preparations for the big feast were going on.

As if a light bulb had gone on over his head, Johnnie said, "Why don't you stay for Thanksgiving dinner? We'd *love* to have you."

"Thank you, but we have reservations at a restaurant in St. Michaels."

Another small group of people arrived, carrying a jug of wine and a bottle of Gray Goose vodka. Introductions, handshakes, and hugs all around. Johnnie gave Bill an affectionate tickle on the shoulder.

Ever the thoughtful host, Johnnie asked if we needed to use the restroom.

"Oh, yes please," my bladder and I responded.

Through the kitchen and a utility room we went, and into a closet sized bathroom.

When I rejoined Kevin and Johnnie, Johnnie said with glee, "Now for the room where the Gulf War was planned."

We walked past a couple of young ladies playing Scrabble and into a sunroom.

"Right here!" Johnnie announced. "They sat *right in this room* and strategized!"

"Wow, that's really something," I said. Then, "We don't want to keep you any longer from your guests. We'll be on our way."

"Oh, *please* let me show you the grounds."

I was cold but agreed to tour the property.

"You can bring your fishing poles and fish from the dock. Take a nap in the hammock. Or you can meditate at the foot of the cross. We've had some *amazing* experiences here. I just listen to the Lord and do what he tells me."

"Wow."

He walked us back to our car where Mia was happy to see us. We weren't allowed to let her out, the property being part of a bird sanctuary. Never mind that Mia's short little bowlegs couldn't chase down a bird if she tried.

Johnnie thrust a pile of brochures at us to give to our friends and family. With waves and promises to come back, we were off. We stopped at the Chesapeake Bay Diner for a bowl of clam chowder and headed back to our inn that seemed to be a magnet for quirky people. Or maybe that's the case with most B&Bs. We meet interesting characters every time we stay in one.

Resting in our cozy room, Kevin answered a knock on the door. It was Gerald.

"We're hanging out in the lobby if you want to join us."

"I'm watching the last quarter of the New England Patriots, my favorite team."

Gerald looked crestfallen.

The Patriots won the game, and Kevin said, "I'll go on out and socialize."

"Not me. I'm staying in the room."

I could hear a lot of talking, male voices through the walls, but couldn't detect the conversation.

After about an hour, Kevin returned and said, "I set Gerald straight on a few things. By the way, they have dinner reservations at the same restaurant we do."

"Uh-oh."

"Theirs is an hour later."

"Whew."

We dressed to the degree that we considered the "smart casual" required, according to its website, by the restaurant we had chosen from the three or four open for Thanksgiving dinner. The hostess seated us on a banquette that curved around a round table next to a window. The view must have been gorgeous during the daytime.

A good-looking guy wearing black from head to toe, as all the wait staff did, said, "Hi. I'm Jim, and I'll be your server this evening. Can I get you something to drink?"

Kevin ordered a ginger ale. He has chosen to abstain from alcohol since his outpatient gall bladder surgery turned into a ten-day hospital stay.

Jim looked at me. "Ma'am?"

I startled Kevin, myself, and perhaps the waiter when I said, "I'll have a Manhattan. Straight up."

Normally I'm not much of a drinker, either. It just kind of popped out of my mouth. I didn't really enjoy it. Way too harsh with bourbon, although the maraschino cherry was good.

Halfway through our meal, Jim reported that Gerald said to tell us they'd arrived.

"Will they be sitting near us?" asked Kevin.

"No, they're at the other end of the dining room."

Okay! I thought.

Next morning, Friday, two more people had joined our little group of holiday revelers—a fellow originally from Switzerland who was now in reverse mortgages at Wells Fargo, and his wife or lady friend. They were an attractive couple, probably also in their sixties. We breakfasted with them in the main dining room while Gerald sounded off about the state of the TSA searches. I overheard Gerald and Soren start a bit of a heated debate on the subject, and was so glad we were in the next room.

Once again, the Russian lady was decked out in her chef's outfit, and served a delicious soufflé with ham and a fruit cup.

I asked our breakfast companion lady what kinds of activities she was involved in.

"Just being with him," she shrugged and pointed to her partner.

"How nice," I said. "I'd like to just be."

Kevin looked at me. "Well. You could you know."

"Nah. I don't think just being is in my DNA."

Come to think of it, maybe it's a learned behavior. Hmm. Time to acquire a new skill.

We packed up and prepared to leave. Kevin was carrying a bag given to him by the Pilots Association when he retired from the Merchant Marines. The bag has a spiffy Federal River Boat Pilots logo on the side, and Gerald was impressed.

"That's so cool! Where'd you get it?"

"Told you I was a Merchant Marine captain. It was a gift when I retired."

"So cool!"

On the way home, Kevin and I were laughing and chatting about our trip, when suddenly behind us appeared a car with flashing blue lights. Oh, crap. Kevin pulled over. The most down-to-business state trooper in the world walked to the window.

"You were clocked doing sixty-eight in a fifty-five."

"Sorry officer. I was running my mouth and didn't realize I was speeding."

He handed over his license and registration. We waited while the trooper checked for outstanding warrants or whatever. Finding none, he walked back and handed Kevin a ticket along with his papers.

"You can send a check for ninety dollars to the State of Maryland." Without another word, he walked away. We saw the same trooper giving two more speeding tickets in the next few minutes. That cop was determined to increase the Maryland state coffers.

Did I mention that on our return home from a bed-and-breakfast Thanksgiving in Asheville, North Carolina, a few years ago, Kevin got a speeding ticket in Emporia, Virginia? Well, he did. I do hope that won't become another of our traditions.

"Please use your cruise control, dear," I said.

Epilogue

Sweet are the uses of adversity
Which, like the toad, ugly and venomous,
Wears yet a precious jewel in his head;
And this our life, exempt from public haunt,
Finds tongues in trees, books in the running brooks,
Sermons in stones, and good in everything.

—*As You Like It,* act 2, scene 1

And so it is. A precious jewel, my life with Kevin, was granted to me after I had suffered almost unbearable adversities. Kevin and I continue to live surrounded by flower gardens, encircled by tall trees in the house that Tim and I built more than twenty years ago. I left the house for a time, after Tim's death, and stayed with his niece in Virginia Beach.

When I was ready to move back, I had the house smudged. Smudging is a powerful spiritual cleansing technique, a legacy from the Native Americans. Those who advocate smudging teach that the smoke attaches itself to negative energy, and, as the smoke clears, the negativity is released. I believe that the negative energy left by the suicide was overwhelmed by the positives of the life Tim and I had had together and by the smudging ceremony. I moved back into my house and enjoy it more every day.

Kevin and I have remodeled and redecorated the house. We've redesigned the gardens, and he, who spent most of his adult years at sea where there are no forests or flowerbeds, turned out to have a very green thumb! Here in our woodland paradise, we live our peaceful and grateful life in the shadow of trees whose eternally reliable strong branches tower and arc over the earth. Arcing as Norman arches rise over an empty medieval cathedral or as the ceiling of the Sistine Chapel towers over men, women, and children in another part of the world.

Often I feel that the spirits of the girls and Tim are with us, cheering us on. Kevin has sensed their presence, too. I've even talked to my daughters during times of meditation and altered consciousness.

I asked Heather, "What would you be like, now, at forty?"

An answer came. "It doesn't matter. I was never forty. I had twelve years with you, but I'm older than you can imagine."

~

There's a legend in the Jewish mystical tradition about unborn children. According to the legend, an angel teaches infants in the womb what their mission on the earth will be. Just before they are born, the angel touches them above the upper lip so they won't remember what he told them until their death. This touch creates the philtrum, the cleft, between the upper lip and nose.

Heart wrenching as it was, I learned to accept that my

daughters lived as long as they needed to on this earth to accomplish their souls' missions.

~

In a reverie, an inner dialogue, I asked Holly years after she died, "Did you know you were not going to come out of that surgery? Were you ready to die? Or was it all random?"

Holly responded in my mind, "No, Mom. There has been nothing random about any of this, hard as that is to believe and to understand for you. Nothing is random. This we know. Some choices are more consciously made than others. But we always, without fail, choose. My personality and my ego did not choose to have cystic fibrosis. Cystic fibrosis was a physical expression of the soul's choice, and it played out through my personality and my body."

"Hmmm," I murmured. "Okay. Now please tell me, when you were in the coma, were you evaluating your options about whether to return to the world with your set of transplanted lungs? Is that what you did for those twelve days?"

"Not so much was I, Holly as personal ego, evaluating, although believe me, Holly as ego had questioned the implications and hardship of living with a transplanted organ. You know I had."

"Yes. I shut out your doubts from my mind, because my grieving heart couldn't fathom your uncertainties."

Holly continued, "And you know I was absolutely opposed to you and Dad sharing your lungs with me. I didn't want you to make that sacrifice for me. I knew that you would eventually understand why it was time for me to leave."

"Were you simply tired of the struggle to live as a vibrant young woman when breathing came so hard?"

"Partly. But more than that, my soul had accomplished its mission. When I was there with you on the earth, I didn't consciously know my mission. Pay attention, Mom. I said I didn't *consciously* know the mission. My soul always knew it, and when I got my ego out of the way, or more accurately when the surgery got my ego out of the way, I knew why I had come to you.

"This may be difficult, but remember that nothing is ever meant to hurt you. Experiences of our lives are meant to make us grow into the beings that are created in the image and after the likeness of the Divinity. I had to teach you to love purely, without strings or conditions. You are a bereaved mother, but you are richly blessed, because you've learned to love wholly and unconditionally."

"I can hardly believe you're telling me this. I don't see the evidence of it." I couldn't breathe quite right as I engaged in this dialogue with one of my dead daughters. My heart pounded, and my solar plexus whirled with strange energies as I remembered the legend about the philtrum.

Then I asked, "Where is Heather? Is she with you?"

"We're not attached at the hip. We don't even have hips."

"You never did. Sorry, Sweetie, I just had to say that."

"Very funny, Mom."

I smiled, amused at the joke I'd made about my two skinny little girls.

"But oh my, didn't you have strong, sturdy well-muscled legs? Oh yes, your dancer's legs and feet were gorgeous."

I remembered Holly's dancing days, her talent, her stage presence and musicality. Then I understood how one of my poem-prayers had been answered.

A few months after Heather's death in 1982, the Tidewater Ballet dedicated a performance to her memory. The lead dancer was a local girl just Heather's age, who went on to become a principal in the New York City Ballet. Later that night, as I popped a strawberry into my mouth at a reception given for the dancers, this poem began to formulate in my mind:

Remembering Heather . . . After the Ballet

She twirls and pointes and pirouettes . . .
while you—you are spirit teardrops on wild honeysuckle.
I see a pas de deux in Celebration . . .
But you—you are spirits' breath in sweet rustling leaves.
Big eyes and pert little face . . . just like you.
She's thirteen now . . . just like you . . .
Would be.
Do you have freckles in Heaven?
  Please God . . .
    This frail fragile creature . . .
    Strong Spirit . . .
    Old soul . . .
    Let her have
    strong legs
    strong lungs
    vibrant life
    To dance in Celebration.
  Under hot lights she leaps and laughs . . .
  While you—you are spirits' wings in a butterfly bush.
  A delicate beautiful bright luminescence
  Glowing throughout the garden's glory.

One of my daughters answered my prayer-poem on behalf of the other, for Holly lived long enough and with sufficient health to develop her dancing skills, to train under a superb teacher at the Tidewater Ballet, and to perform with the Governor's Magnet School for the Arts. Leap and laugh she did. With strong vibrant legs, she danced in celebration.

The girls said to me during meditation early one morning, "Your faith in our abilities to participate in life made all the difference to us. Thank you, Mommy, for allowing us and encouraging us to go out into the world and explore.

"Now it's your turn to live joyfully, Mom. Don't ever be afraid to live fully and to give your whole, healed heart."

The broken pieces of my heart have been put back together.

Scarred places, like grouting lines on a treasured mosaic piece, will be with me forever.

But thanks to faith and grace, the shattered shards have been reassembled with new love.

Heather was ten and Holly was six in this picture of us.

Our family of three in 1984; Holly was ten.

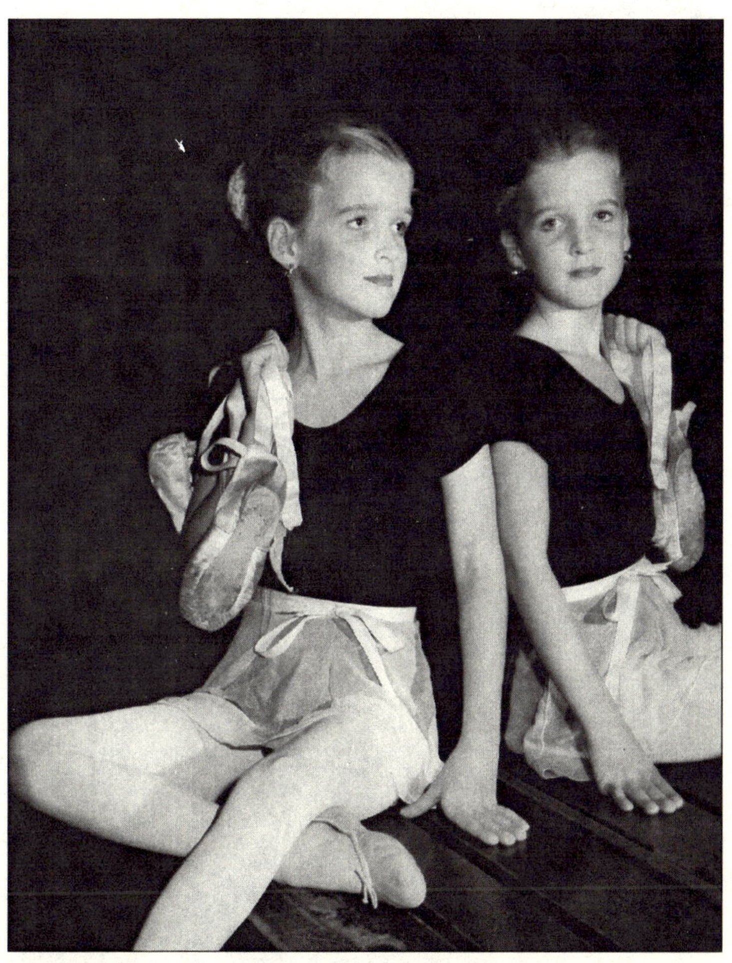

This picture was on the cover of *KidStuff* magazine in 1984; Holly at ten.

Holly, twenty, with Sugar

Heather, twelve,
on New Year's Day 1982

About the Author

Terry Jones-Brady has been an actress and educator and is now an award-winning freelance writer. She holds a bachelors degree from the University of California at Berkeley, a masters degree from Norfolk State University, and is a certified spiritual director. She lives in Virginia with her husband, their English bulldog, and their cockatiel.